CREATIVE GUITAR: WRITING AND PLAYING ROCK SONGS WITH ORIGINALITY

MB21484

BY JEFFREY ROESSNER

"Without deviation progress is not possible."
— Frank Zappa

"Imagining playing the guitar is a slightly looser thing than playing it. You can hear more things sometimes. The fingers of your imagnation aren't quite as hidebound as your real fingers."
— Richard Thompson

TABLE OF CONTENTS

Introduction

Have you ever heard a guitar player live or even on the radio and thought, "Yeah, he's alright. He can clearly *play*. But something's missing"? Some element of excitement or vitality just wasn't there. If you really thought about it, you might decide that the missing element was an original touch, that certain hard-to-define quality that would make his playing his own rather than a note-perfect copy of someone else's style. How different that experience is from Eric Clapton's account of the first time he heard Stevie Ray Vaughan. Listening to the radio when Stevie came on, Clapton wheeled his car to the side of the road and vowed that he had to know who that guitar player was today—not tomorrow, but *today*. Although an extreme example, this story suggests the power of an original player, the kind of guitarist most of us want to be—the kind who stops people in their tracks.

Unfortunately, most guitarists are left on their own in developing a creative approach, especially when it comes to writing a song. Sure, there are hundreds of books about guitar playing, and there are many books about song writing—but there are very few books about writing a rock song on the guitar. What's more, the books on guitar playing generally focus on one thing: improving your technical ability. If you want to master a new scale or learn to emulate the sound of a steel guitar on your Telecaster, that's fine. But it's not the whole story of guitar playing, especially when it comes to writing, arranging, and playing a song with an original style.

This book aims to demystify the craft of composing a rock song on your guitar. As such, it's designed for players of all ages and abilities who want to:

- develop more original ideas for songs
- become unstuck from their current level of playing
- polish songs already written, or take them to the next level
- arrange their original songs for performance or recording

Conventional wisdom would have you believe that such skills are not easily learned: songwriters are either innately gifted or have practiced and perfected their art through years of hard work. Certainly, both of these hold true for many artists, but only to a certain extent. Although there aren't simple rules or a formula that you can easily memorize to produce an original style, that doesn't mean great players begin to write blindly, hoping for divine inspiration to bestow a song on them. In fact, in the pages to come, I will argue just the opposite. Great players definitely have an approach to structuring and arranging their material when they write. By exploring how these artists compose, we can learn from their experience and their example, and apply those lessons to our own compositions. In short, why struggle for years to learn what master songwriters know when we can examine their songs and listen to what they say to speed up the process?

Some might say, though, that creative thinking of any kind cannot be taught. To be creative means in some sense to break the rules, to devise new ways of doing things. How can examining the styles of other artists help *you* be original? The answer becomes clear when we consider the stories of innovative musicians: none simply began by producing a masterpiece. Instead, they generally put serious effort into learning the basic skills, the terminology, and the structure of their art as it has been practiced by those who came before them. Oddly enough, this process doesn't crush your originality, it frees it. Only by knowing what's been done and what works can you understand how to make your unique contribution.

In helping you devise an original approach to songwriting, this book will explore the ideas and principles that guide accomplished writers, and that often seem to work at the level of intuition. In so doing, the book has two aims. First, it explains how composers at work generally think in terms of the major elements of a song: the riff, the verse, the chorus, the solo. We'll examine each of these parts in detail—with many examples—and then discuss how to arrange them for a band. These parts aren't in every song, and you certainly don't have to write or arrange them in the order in which they're covered here. Still, as the examples I'll use demonstrate, these elements are remarkably consistent throughout rock and roll history, from classic sixties groups through contemporary and alternative bands. Second, because it's not enough simply to learn the basic elements of song-craft, the book explores countless examples of rock innovators who adapt, bend, and disregard the rules to suit their particular needs. This part of the book is designed to provide a model of creativity in action—one that you can use in writing your own dynamic, inventive songs.

The examples I'll use are based on the work of well-known artists, and the parts are all represented in tab form. But I've chosen not to include a CD demonstrating the parts for one important reason: the aim of the book is not to encourage you to ape someone else's style, but to help you create your own. In order to do so, each chapter culminates with a series of exercises designed to promote original thinking. Because they invite you to try imaginative new approaches as you compose your own music, the exercises can't really be "learned" in any traditional sense. Consequently, no two guitarists who follow the suggestions will come up with the same music, and in fact, you can return to the exercises again and again without fear of repeating yourself. In short, they are presented to inspire you and help generate novel ideas for writing your own songs in your own style—the ultimate signs of creativity.

Chapter One

Dreaming Your Songs: A Model of Creativity

I don't care about the rules. In fact, if I don't break the rules at least ten times in every song then I'm not doing my job properly
— Jeff Beck

One day in 1965, so the story goes, John Lennon was struggling to come up with a song for the next Beatles' record. For hours he sat and strummed through chord changes and sang bits of lyrics that popped into his head. But nothing gelled; nothing struck him as the song he wanted to write. Feeling tired and frustrated with his lack of progress, he put the guitar down and sank into a reverie. And that's when it happened. Just as he gave up all thoughts of trying to write a song, inspiration struck. He picked up his guitar and out came "Nowhere Man," seemingly fully formed with lyrics and melody.

Why begin with this story? Because it affirms some of the most staunchly held—and debilitating— myths about creativity and music. Lennon's story does highlight the pitfalls of trying to bring a song into being with sheer force of will. But it also works as a parable that confirms his status as a genius, a conduit through which the musical gods chose to express themselves. In short, the moral of the story seems to be that songwriting has little to do with hard work or conscious effort, and everything to do with a magical, unexplainable gift.

Now I'd want to be the last one to suggest that Lennon was not a supremely gifted musician and songwriter. But his tale of composing "Nowhere Man" doesn't seem very useful for those of us trying to learn the craft of songwriting. In fact, it ranks up there with other fabulous tales of songs that apparently arrived from some other world. Paul McCartney claimed that he dreamed the complete melody for "Yesterday," then went around for weeks trying to discover whether he'd actually written it or had unconsciously plagiarized it from a source he couldn't recall. And Keith Richards also tells a good story about writing in his sleep. He claims that he woke up in the middle of the night, recorded the riff that would become the opening for the Stone's anthem, "Satisfaction," then dozed off again. In the morning, he found the tape, played it, and discovered the riff—but he had no memory of actually waking up or composing it.

These stories have become legendary among Stones and Beatles fans—but I don't think that fully explains why they continue to be told. At least in part, these tales fascinate because this is the way we wish things were: we want to believe that brilliant, original songs flow along the stream of inspiration, and all we have to do is set our antennae correctly to pick them up. No uncertainty, no confusion, no difficult decisions to make while writing. In short, these stories are told because they are just that, great stories. And great stories are by definition unusual, unique—*exceptions* to the rule. John, Paul, and Keith didn't dream every song they wrote. If they had relied on this method, you can be sure they would have written far fewer songs.

In fact, if we look a little closer, we can find other songwriting stories that might ring truer to our experience. In the famous *Playboy* interviews given shortly before his death, Lennon dispels the myth that he and Paul wrote their material separately. "We wrote a lot of stuff together, one-on-one, eyeball to eyeball" (150). Such extensive collaboration was necessary, as Lennon goes on to explain that "the demand on us was tremendous" and "we really used to absolutely write like that—both playing into each other's noses. We spent hours and hours and hours…" (150). Stressing the sheer amount of time spent working on the material, Lennon here offers a strikingly different account than the reverie that magically produced "Nowhere Man."

A good description of this writing process occurs in Hunter Davies' book *The Beatles,* the first full-length biography of the band. Offering one of the few eye-witness accounts of the Beatles composing, Davies had a privileged view of Lennon and McCartney at work on several songs, including "With a Little Help From My Friends" and "Getting Better." Davies notes that he showed up for the second day of work on "With a Little Help," as John and Paul tried to hammer out the lyrics. As for "Getting Better," Davies watched the melody and lyrics take basic shape after hours of "playing, singing, improvising, and messing around" (303).

During this period of their career, the general pattern was that John and Paul would convene for a songwriting session at about two o'clock in the afternoon. One or both would bring an idea for part of a song—a bit of melody or a scrap of lyric—and they would work on in through the evening, until they moved the proceedings to the recording studio.

This account explains a few things about the way John and Paul wrote together, and offers a more helpful vision of the writing process. First, it's evident that no matter how easily song ideas came to them, they did not rely on inspiration alone. In the case of "With a Little Help," Davies suggests that it was an ongoing process that lasted at least several days – they had started writing the song well before he got there, and continued to work on it as they prepared to record. Second, this account reveals their dedication to their craft. They scheduled blocks of time to write, and during those sessions, rarely succumbed to frustration. As writers, John and Paul generally refused to get stuck: if some element of the tune or lyric stumped them, they didn't dwell on it. Instead, they would distract themselves briefly by breaking into a corny song—even a Beatle classic—or toying with one of the odd assortment of instruments scattered around them. Then they would just as abruptly fix their attention again on the song, seemingly unflappable in their faith that the details would be ironed out with enough patience.

As Davies presents them, John and Paul work as professional songwriters. They know what elements of the song need to be addressed, they envision how the song as a whole will flow, and they do this together. This last point is especially important: because they work together, sharing ideas, they must also share essential ideas about the structure and direction of the song they're writing. To an outsider, this process might look magical; in fact, it would probably seem to confirm traditional notions of inspiration: because the principles that guide them seem invisible, John and Paul appear to be relying on intuition alone.

But I would argue that most songwriters, especially in stories they tell about themselves, only *appear* to rely solely on inspiration. In fact, they're working with a set of flexible but nonetheless definable guidelines that can be learned. We might think of these guidelines as part of an experienced songwriter's "tacit knowledge," their unspoken assumptions about how to approach composing. These are the unwritten rules that make a professional's work look like magic to a beginner. The most important of these guidelines includes a thorough knowledge of how songs have traditionally been structured—in other words, the "parts" such as riff, chorus, and bridge that make up a rock song. With some variation or other, these elements appear in virtually every rock song ever written, from classics by the Who, Bob Dylan, and Led Zeppelin, through various alternative songs by Nirvana, Stone Temple Pilots, and Sarah McLaughlin.

How can an emphasis on these "traditional" song structures lead to originality or innovation? Why—in order to write or play an innovative piece of music—do you need to understand the basic structure of a rock song built around the guitar? For several reasons. Mainly because without this understanding, you won't know whether your song is strikingly original or merely a collection of clichés. Using feedback in a guitar solo was a creative breakthrough for Jimi Hendrix. But if you do it now in a similar manner, you're just someone aping *his* style. Likewise, starting a song with the chorus rather than the verse might sound unique, but do you know how often it's been done?

In a sense, then, the knowledge of song structure is like the background you would need to be an innovator in any field. Legend has it that Albert Einstein wasn't gifted in mathematics. But it would be foolish to underestimate the thorough grounding in physics that allowed him to formulate his theories. In other words, average guys with little training in their field generally don't simply sit down one day and decide to innovate—just as Stevie Ray Vaughan didn't just pick up his guitar one day and decide to be original. That's why, without some understanding of how songs have been put together in the past, you aren't likely to consistently produce fresh and exciting material.While this emphasis on traditional structure is crucial, however, it is only the first part of the equation of creativity.

Along with understanding the patterns in rock songwriting, you need to develop a feel for how players and songs have stretched, broken, or re-written the "rules" in creative ways. In other words, one way to learn to innovate is to study the innovations of others. To do this, you need to look at countless examples of songs as models of original writing and playing. You must explore what elements have made a song or guitar part unique, because at some point you have to go beyond the rules. The exercises below and throughout the book offer examples of how others achieved originality, inspiration for trying new things, tips for getting unstuck in the process of songwriting, and advice on arranging your music. In short, they are designed to spark your imagination as you develop your own style and sound.

Finally, if we've learned one thing from studying creativity, it's that the great innovators in any field do share a common trait: they make lots of mistakes. A leading researcher on creativity, Dean Simonton notes that the inventor Thomas Edison held over one thousand patents, most of which are worthless. To be original, you have to try new things, and when we first attempt something, we often fall down. Think about learning to ride a bike or trying to master a new riff on your guitar. Usually, we're not very graceful in these situations. So write lots of songs. Everyday pick up your guitar with the intention of composing something new. And remember, by the time the Beatles signed a record contract, John and Paul were already claiming that they'd written one hundred songs together.

Exercises

1) While I have been emphasizing the steady work of professional songwriters, don't take this as the one way you should write a song. Everyone writes differently. Paul Simon goes to his office to write on schedule, and Keith Richards maintains that he simply can't understand that approach. In fact, Richards seems firmly committed to his "inspirational" model, and writes only when the spirit moves him. These extremes suggest the sheer variety of approaches to songwriting out there.

I suspect, though, that you'll write more and better songs if you remain committed to steady work on the song rather than waiting for divine inspiration (which somehow seems to come sporadically and rarely when you want it). But go easy on yourself for your approach and experiment with new tactics as you discover what works best for you.

2) One good way of honing your skills is to pay close attention to the interviews in which guitarists talk about their songwriting. How do they describe their writing process? Do they use mystical terms? Try not to take the stories about writing all at face value: do they describe writing every song this way? Or are they simply telling good stories? And again, note how each player describes the process differently.

3) Start examining the structure of your favorite songs. How does the song open? What is it about the song that first grabs your attention? Is the guitar line, the melody, the sound? Then look at the arrangement of the song. How are the verses, solos, and choruses put together? Does the chorus come first? Does the solo simply replace the verse, or does the solo occur over new changes or in a different key? Examining song structure in this way will help you expand your vision of possible ways to construct your own songs.

4) Check out books that offer good insights into how musicians craft their songs. I've already mentioned *The Playboy Interviews* with John Lennon and Hunter Davies' *The Beatles*, but there are countless other sources. One good one is *Written on My Soul: Conversations with Rock's Great Songwriters* by Bill Flanagan. Also, of course, read the biographies of your favorite bands. And if you want more specific and technical guitar tips, pick up a copy of *Secrets from the Masters,* a collection of interviews from the vaults of *Guitar Player* magazine. In it, great players talk about their practice strategies and how they arrive at ideas for songs and solos. Finally, check out the "Further Reading" appendix at the end of this book for more suggestions on inspiring books about songwriting and creativity.

5) Keeping in mind the story of Thomas Edison's one thousand patents, adopt the goal of writing songs all the time. Each time you pick up the guitar, invent something: a riff, a chord change, a new position for a

chord, a melody for a solo, etc. Don't worry whether or not the part is brilliant; who says you have to be a genius all the time? Remember, the only way to get better at anything is through practice.

When developing your creative skills, you'll discover that it requires a different kind of attention and focus than when you're practicing a scale. Take the time to notice how you think and feel when you're composing rather than doing guitar drills. Cultivate that mindset.

6) Set a goal for yourself of writing one song every day for a week.

Chapter Two

The Riff: Devising a Stunning Opener

*My vocation is more in composition really than anything else—building up
harmonies using the guitar, orchestrating the guitar like an army, a guitar army.*
— Jimmy Page

Think back to the last concert you attended. Can you remember a song that, within the first few bars—sometimes with the first chord—instantly had everyone clapping and stomping? That response was from the song's hook, and it was most likely played on a guitar.

By now the term "hook" in a pop song has been celebrated, mythologized, and finally denigrated. Mention that you need a hook for your song, and it instantly conjures the image of a pudgy, balding record executive in a polyester leisure suit whining, "Sure, it's a good song, but where's the *hook*?" As if the opening riff of a song were solely connected to the bottom line. As if there were actually something wrong with catching the listener's attention, or with playing a riff that made the song instantly recognizable.

Despite the objections, there seems to be no getting away from it—a good, memorable song often starts with an ear-catching riff designed to snag your attention and keep it.

If you still doubt the importance of the opening run, just think of the masters of creating such riffs. How difficult is it to hum the opening bars of your favorite song? Probably not a challenge, and that's what great players have known for a long time. Take Jimmy Page, for example. There's no question that he's a brilliant soloist, and a fantastic arranger and producer. But his legacy rests in large part on the indelible hooks he created for his band. An amazing number of Led Zeppelin songs begin with an unforgettable riff—and usually one that's not too complex: "Whole Lotta Love," "Black Dog," "Heartbreaker," "Dazed and Confused." The list could include just about any Zeppelin tune. In fact, one criticism of Page might be that sometimes the opening riff is *all* that he writes. The whole song often stretches out under that hypnotic, riveting guitar intro.

Let's look at some examples of effective riffs and see how they're designed to instantly grab your attention and set the tone for the song to come.

Single Note Riffs

Offering one of the most recognizable intros in rock history, Jimi Hendrix's "Purple Haze" establishes a pattern that you'll see used repeatedly for a song's opening. It begins with a two-bar octave riff (B flat notes) played on each punching beat over the snare drum, then Hendrix launches into the famous four-note run that serves as the song's calling card. Here's a riff similar to that opening:

Example 2.1

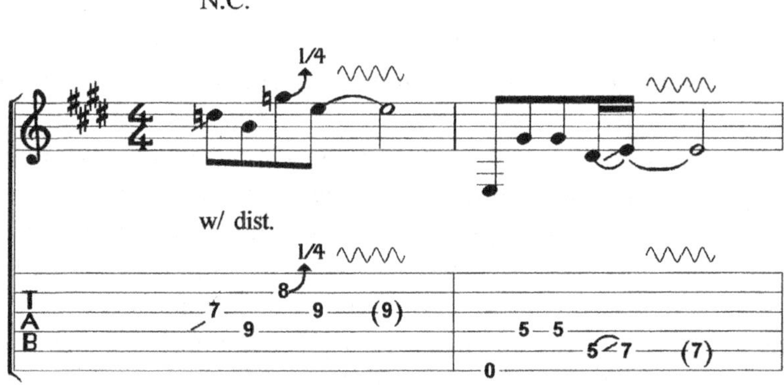

The run here is played so fluidly it's almost as though he's improvising it. In fact, the lick has a call-and-response structure that's in many ways closer to jazz than to rock. Hendrix first plays the opening riff, then answers it with a parallel four-note run on the lower strings, mimicking the rhythm of the opening. Then he does it all over again, before beginning a series of variations on that main theme in the following manner:

Example 2.2

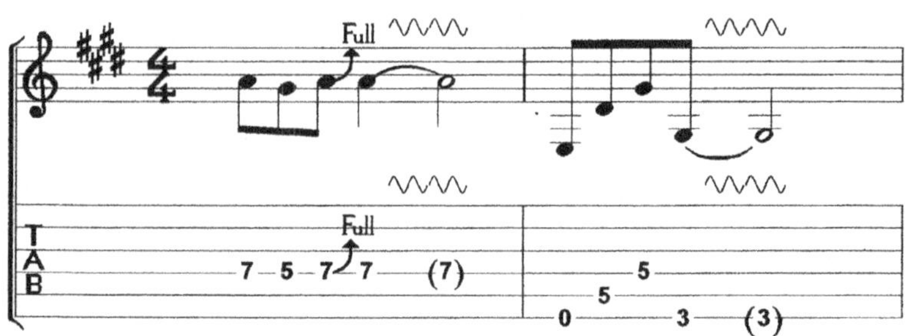

After completing runs in this style, he tags on a brief ascending riff that carries us to the first chords of the verse. Not an extremely difficult intro to play, but one that does an effective job at setting the stage for the rest of the song.

The first point to note is that the riff is there solely to open the song—in other words, Hendrix never sings over it, and he only reprises it later (after the solo). So at its most basic, the hook serves this essential purpose, to provide a catchy opening. Second, although the riff is relatively basic—relying on four-note licks not played at lighting speed—it announces the tonality of the song. The verse begins on an E7#9 chord, not a very typical one in rock music (you can also here it during the verse of the Beatles' "Taxman").

Hendrix essentially builds the riff on the key tones in this chord. In other words, he offers an arresting opening because he's avoided simply relying the notes of an E major chord (E, G#, B). Instead, he takes the relatively unusual E7#9 chord and shapes a lick based on its distinctive tones (E ,G#, B, D, G) . The wider harmonic range of this extended chord lends itself to a more complex and interesting riff. Hendrix also, by the way, jars our ears at the very outset with the octave riff that serves as a kind of intro to the intro. This riff uses A# notes—a startling choice since the rest of tune is in the key E (which does not include an A#). In essence, he shifts to a different key after the brief octave riff.

Here's a guitar line modeled after the beginning of Led Zeppelin's "Living Loving Maid (She's Just a Woman)" as an example of another kind of introduction, and the sort of heavy riffing Jimmy Page is known for. Note that the part is actually comprised of two guitars playing the same line, one an octave above the other. Not too complicated or fancy, but definitely reminiscent of Page's signature licks:

Example 2.4

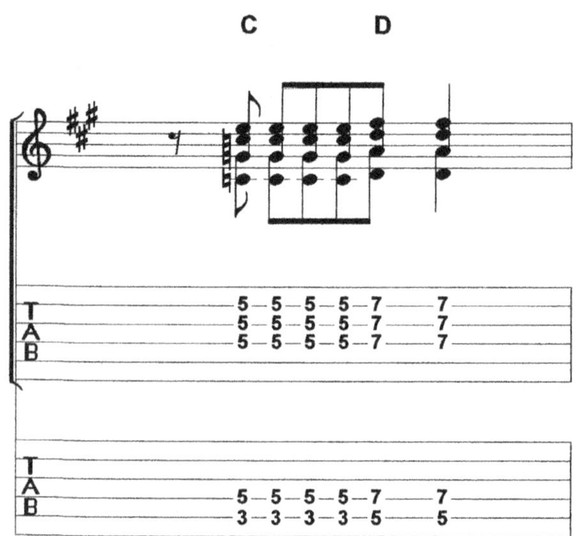

In "Living Loving Maid," Page's riff occurs at the opening, between lyrics in the verses, and finally at the end of the tune. You can begin to see then how it helps define an essential quality of the song. It's not just a gimmicky opening designed to catch your attention—although a riff certainly can be that, too. But in important ways, it sets the tone for the song to come by establishing the rhythm, the key, and the tempo.

Page's opening for "Living, Loving, Maid" signals that the song is in the key of A, and sets up a persistent, driving beat—the riff sounds almost impatient, and that's clearly part of what makes it so catchy. Finally, it also allows the band to call attention to the bridge and the solo sections of the song as they break the pace of the opening. As Page moves to the solo, for example, the song shifts to a chord sequence (D-A-D-E) whose simple rhythm sets it apart and gives the listener a slight relief from tension built up in the initial driving beat. Finally, because it recurs throughout, the riff in many ways ties the tune together: you expect to hear it played, and if the song didn't return to it, you would somehow feel cheated.

Chord Riffs

Of course, some might complain that Page's single-note riffs are bombastic, excessive—a throwback to the bloated, over-produced rock of the 1970s. But it's important to keep in mind that the hook does not have to be a single note run in the manner of classics such as The Rolling Stones' "Satisfaction" or The Beatles' "Day Tripper." Play this chord and see if you can identify the song it opens:

Example 2.5

Recognize it as the first chord in The Beatles' "A Hard Day's Night"? Most rock fans will. Here, the Beatles managed to reduce the hook to one chord.

Obviously, the riff doesn't have to be quite as sparse as in "A Hard Day's Night." But there are a surprising number of ways to construct a compelling opening with chords as an alternative to single-note runs. John Fogerty, for example, continually relied on chord riffs in the songs he wrote for Creedence Clearwater Revival. Let's look at an opening similar to one of his most famous songs, "Bad Moon Rising." Note how straightforward this chord change is—and how Fogerty crafts an unforgettable opening from a similar run.

Example 2.6

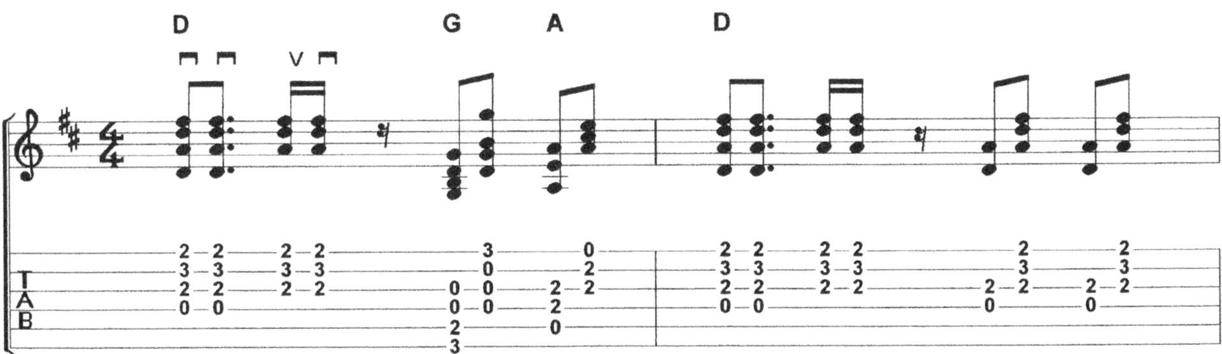

As a slight variation to this, Fogerty often employed a basic chord riff with a guitar run over the top of it. In this example, akin to "Who'll Stop the Rain," you pick notes out of the basic chords as you freely strum a G to Em change:

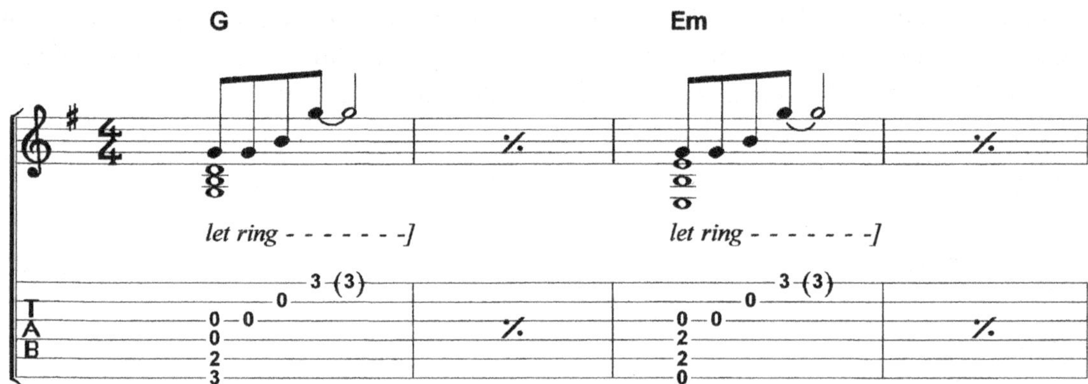

In "Who'll Stop the Rain," Fogerty's brilliance shines through in the way that he seems to distill the riff down to a bare essence. Basically, you don't have to do anything special with your fretting hand besides planting it on the chords. Still, this serves the main purposes of the opening. It certainly is recognizable, and it reflects the rootsy, playing-on-the-front-porch feel for which he's known.

Fingerpicking Good

Another distinctive and long successful approach for opening a song is with fingerpicking. The gentler, more responsive tone produced by the fleshy pads of the fingers can help set a unique mood for a tune. This technique has been used on a number of rock classics, including everything from Led Zeppelin's gothic "Stairway to Heaven" to the folky musings of James Taylor. But as we'll see, it's not simply an old-fashioned or dated style of playing. In fact, several contemporary artists have plucked their way to distinction.

Because there are countless fingerstyle patterns you can employ on a song, let's look at a few examples that represent the sheer range of styles available. The first one comes from John Lennon's work with the Beatles. While studying meditation in India in the late 1960s, Lennon learned a new fingerstyle pattern from the folk singer Donovan. This happy encounter quickly resulted in the composition of three songs for the *White Album* ("Dear Prudence," "Happiness is a Warm Gun," and "Julia") as well as a number of tunes he would write later, in his solo career.

Note that learning one fairly simple picking technique spurred Lennon to compose several now-classic songs. It's as if every guitar part he learned became a possible source of inspiration. That's a powerful reminder of why it's important to keep practicing and keep learning from other guitarists.

Here's the fingerpicking pattern that Lennon learned from Donovan, used to play a very basic C to Am change. When practicing this riff, keep in mind that the notes on the A and low E strings should be played with the thumb, while all higher strings are plucked with your fingers.

Example 2.8

If you're not well-versed in fingerstyle technique, you'll quickly notice that it takes a strong left hand and good right-hand finger coordination to articulate the notes and stay in rhythm. This will take practice, especially at the beginning as you try to master the basic fingering. The best advice is to break the part in two. Start by playing the bass parts (or "thumb" notes) until you're comfortable with them, then you can begin to add the higher parts. Always start slow: play the pattern in a very methodical way and establish the rhythm at a snail's pace. Once you grasp how it feels to pick this way (and your fingers have memorized the pattern), you'll be able to play it rapidly with very little effort. At that point, you can sit back and let your fingers do their stuff.

If you want use this pattern to understand the beginning of "Julia," simply add a capo at the second fret and play a C-Am-Em-G progression. The opening of "Happiness is a Warm Gun" uses more compelling chords, including the following:

Example 2.9

Once you've mastered the basic pattern, experiment by using it with a variety of other chords. You'll see how great it sounds and why it led to such a songwriting bonanza for Lennon.

The second fingerpicking example we'll consider is in the style of one of the most distinctive songwriters to emerge in the past decade, Sheryl Crow. She composes songs that showcase innovative guitar work, including everything from unusual open tunings to slide work. To top it off, she's a multi-instrumentalist who often writes and plays the six-string parts herself. It's not surprising, then, that when she decides to employ fingerpicking, the result is both tasteful and strikingly original. Here's a riff in the style of "Strong Enough." In Crow's song, her run both opens the song and carries the verses.

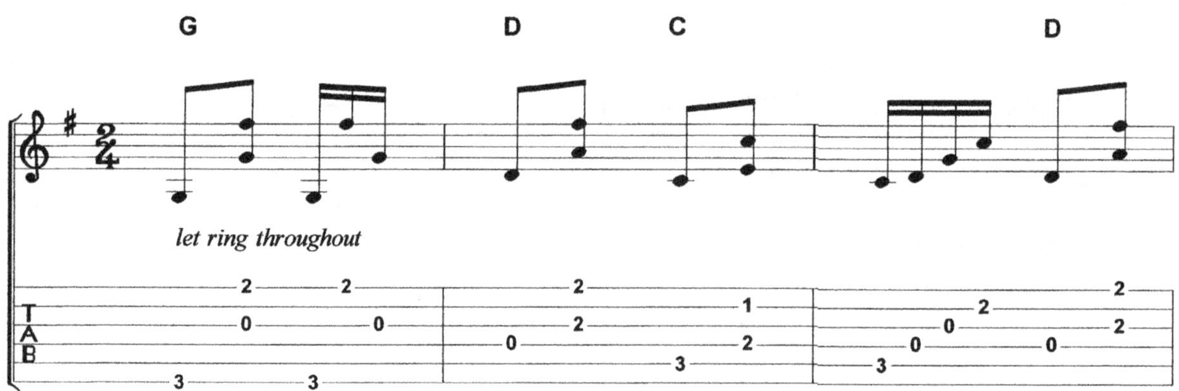

As in "Strong Enough," my original example here employs a fairly standard picking technique, alternating thumb and fingers, which provides bass notes to keep the rhythm and higher tones to reinforce the melody. Within the pattern, though, the part moves into original territory with the run based on the C chord that leads back to the beginning of the riff. This is the most challenging part to play clearly. To master it, you need to remember to remove your middle finger from the open C shape, and make sure to arch your ring finger enough to let the D note resonate.

It's important to play this C chord lick clearly because it gives the part its unusual, complex harmony. The D note sounds unsettled because it's not part of the C triad (C-E-G). In "Strong Enough," Crow achieves a similar, striking effect by adding a G note to a Bm triad (B-D-F#) as she plays through the changes to the song (D-G-Bm-A). Notice how such a simple touch—the addition of one distinctive note—catches your ear and helps establish a somber mood for the song.

Once you've mastered this fingerpicking pattern, experiment with it using different keys and different, unique chords. As Crow's example shows, even basic chords, if they're approached from an original angle, can be made as striking as the flashiest riff.

While Crow demonstrates the soulful flavor of acoustic fingerpicking, John Frusciante's work with the Red Hot Chili Peppers enters the terrain of jazzy psychedelia. A versatile stylist and truly innovative player, Frusciante has employed fingerpicking on some of his band's best known tracks, including "Under the Bridge" and "Scar Tissue." On these songs, he sets up dramatic contrast between the picking he uses in the intro and verses and the strumming in the choruses.

But more important, Frusciante rescues a tone that many rock players ignore: the sweet sound of fingerpicking on an electric guitar. While jazz players have never underestimated the appeal of this technique, rock guitarists invariably reach for the acoustic when called on to play without a pick. This can be a serious miscalculation, as Frusciante demonstrates. Here's a riff in the style of "Scar Tissue," which should be played with a slightly distorted tone reminiscent of Hendrix.

Example 2.11

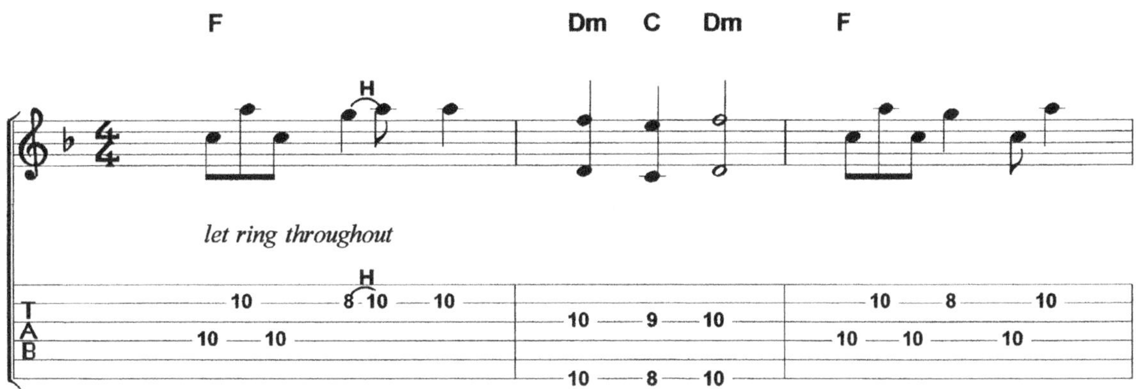

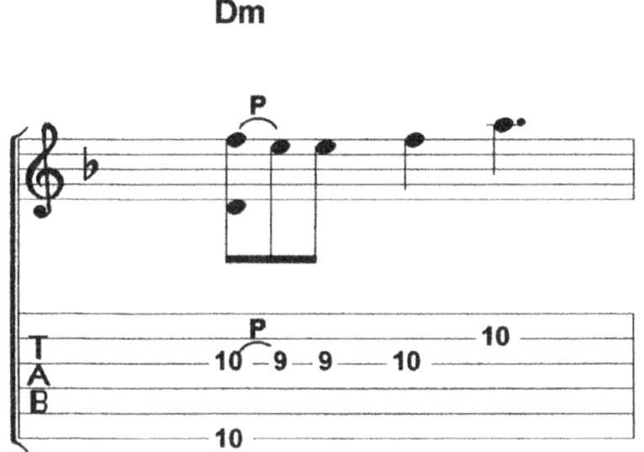

Although it might take some practice to coordinate all the effects in this part, it's worth the effort. Notice how the example can be played with only two fingers of your right hand, the thumb and index finger. Only two fingers—again, consider how economy and simplicity work for this part. Also, note how the hammer-on and the pull-off add sophistication to a fairly straightforward pattern. With fingerpicking, nuance is crucial. Even if your picking pattern and your chords are fairly basic, a deft use of left-hand techniques can help you forge a signature lick. As always, after you master this run, try playing variations of it with new intervals and different accents, including slides, hammer-ons, pull-offs.

The three song examples here show the diverse effects possible with fingerpicking. Whether it's a fairly standard pattern that you adapt ("Julia" and "Happiness is a Warm Gun") or an utterly original part you devise ("Strong Enough" and "Scar Tissue"), keep searching until you discover or create the lick that works for your song.

Alternative Hooks?

No matter what anyone says, contemporary songs—even by so-called alternative bands—have not given up the hook. They may downplay the overblown, slickly produced riffs with twelve guitar overdubs, but these bands usually still offer an opening run that identifies the song and signals its direction.

Nirvana's "All Apologies" immediately comes to mind. This simple riff can be played by almost anyone who has literally just picked up the guitar. But I know that when I first heard it, it lodged in my head like it had been shot there with a nail gun. There's simply no getting around the catchiness of it. One sure test of this is that after you've heard it, you wonder why someone hadn't thought of it before. Here's a riff that employs the same ringing tone that Cobain used for "All Apologies" (note that Cobain tuned down one-half a step to E flat on his song):

Example 2.12

This is a good example of an alternative to a bombastic, single-note riff. It relies on droning bass notes played on the low E string (this kind of open, ringing note is called a "pedal tone") while the fretting hand slides around creating different intervals on the higher strings. Cobain's guitar approach clearly owes a debt to the rise of college radio in the mid-1980s and the return to jangly pop sounds by bands such as R.E.M. For precursors to the "All Apologies" riff, listen to R.E.M.'s "Seven Chinese Brothers" or "Talk About the Passion." Like Cobain, Peter Buck relied heavily on catchy rhythmic phrases, and he often picked out notes within basic chord shapes.

Other more contemporary bands have in fact signaled a return to an earlier era when a crunchy chord riff set the stage for a song. Played with sizzling distortion and emphasizing a low-fi sound, Hole's "Celebrity Skin" and Veruca Salt's "Seether" are prime examples of such chord-based intros. Here are riffs in the vein of these two bands:

Example 2.13

Example 2.14

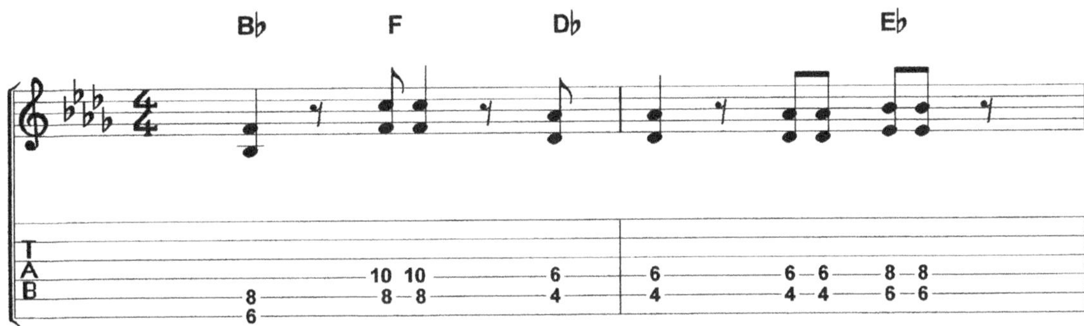

How far are these from the raunchy opening of the Kink's sixties classics "All Day and All of the Night" or "You Really Got Me"? The production values here might seem more anti-commercial—with the seemingly out of control vocal delivery or the lurch into pop sweetness for the bridge in "Celebrity Skin"—but these bands are very much in a spirited, back-to-basics rock tradition where that all-mighty power chord drives the song.

Of course, there are countless ways to build an opening for a song: a cappella singing, drums, piano, orchestra—all have been tried in some variation or another, and we'll explore these ideas further in the chapter on arranging your song. But if you turn on the radio or flip to MTV, you'll hear many songs that still rely on that old stand-by, the trusty six-string guitar. Sometimes it's detuned, sometimes distorted almost beyond recognition, sometimes without all of its strings—or with more strings—but it's still a guitar used to provide the opening tones of a song.

Here are some exercises to try when devising the opening for your original tune.

Exercises

1) If you want to write a great riff, start by paying attention to the openings of your favorite songs. What is the first thing that strikes you about the intro riff? How complicated is the riff? How fast is it played? How many guitar parts are used on it? After studying a few songs in this way, consider how you might apply some of those techniques to your own tunes. Obviously, if you're attracted to hard rock licks played at blistering speed, then that's the kind of riff you want to shoot to compose. The main point is to become more aware of what you like in a guitar riff. In doing so, you'll gain a sharper sense of the kind of riff you want to write.

2) Like Jimmy Page in "Living, Loving Maid," many guitarists have doubled their guitar parts an octave higher. Jimi Hendrix is famous for this, although he often used an octave pedal to achieve the effect – you can hear it in the run he plays just after singing "'Scuze me while I kiss the sky" and in the solo for "Purple Haze." The Beatles' "Birthday" relies on a similar strategy.

Try writing a single note run that can be doubled with another guitar playing an octave higher. Avoid focusing on making it complicated or clever. Just pick a note to start on and play around until you hit on a tuneful lick. As you begin to come up with ideas for the run, see if you can develop a rhythm or beat for it, and let that help dictate what notes you'll play.

Finally, get another guitarist to play along, supplying one of the lines. Alternatively, you can simply tape the riff and play along with it in another octave, or use a foot-pedal to achieve the effect. You'll be surprised at how full and how unique the part sounds when you double it this way.

3) Instead of a single note run, explore ways of opening the song with a single, unique chord. You might thumb through a chord dictionary for the guitar and see what you discover. Once you have an interesting chord, you can then decide how it will fit into the opening of the song—will you simply play the chord, or can you use the notes in it as the basis for a riff? If you're stuck, think of the examples from Hendrix and Fogerty, and remember to keep it simple at first. The riff doesn't need to be too clever, just memorable.

4) Write a chord change that you can play that will identify your song. Here you'll want more than simply a distinctive single chord; instead, focus on developing a riff composed of two, three, or four chords. For starters, try basic chords such as E, A, and D and make the rhythm the distinguishing feature of the song.

You might then expand the range by playing chords not usually put together in a key (if you're not clear on this, don't worry, we'll discuss it in depth in the next chapter). For example, you might include an A chord in the middle of a C-G-D change, and note how your riff gains harmonic force by the unexpected combination. In short, experiment with your own songs by adding an unusual or surprising chords to the mix.

5) Try writing a crunchy chord riff in the classic rock style. Look at the examples in the style of Hole and Veruca Salt and note how low-tech these licks can be. When you're writing, try to establish a heavy rhythm— that's the force that drives the song, after all. The chords themselves can be simple (comprised of just a root and the fifth), but you can also make them more interesting if you like. Try playing the root and the third or flatted third: for example, instead of playing a G and D note to form the G chord, use a G and a B or B flat. The key is to experiment, and try everything you can think of until you hit on what sounds good to you.

6) Write a riff using an opening pedal tone like the one in Nirvana's "All Apologies" or any of the R.E.M. songs discussed above. Keep in mind that it doesn't have to start on the low E String. In fact, you could devise a run that employs a high open string. You might, for example, use the high E as your constant note while you slide to different notes on the B string. Whichever string you use for the pedal tone, be sure to preserve a ringing or droning quality—that's the distinguishing feature of this technique.

7) Try inventing a lick from the shape of one or two basic chords in the manner of "Who'll Stop the Rain." You might consider using a capo to change the flavor of the open notes that you play. Feel free to add notes outside the chord(s) if they add depth or complexity to your riff.

8) John Fogerty tells an instructive story about writing his classic tune "Proud Mary." He claims that he was listening to Beethoven's Fifth Symphony and trying to play the opening on his guitar. This is the famous symphony that opens with that instantly recognizable "Da-Da-Da Duuummm." Now think about that rhythm in relation to Fogerty's song, and consider how he took that phrase and extended the ending.

When you're trying to come up with ideas for a song, listen to another form of music not closely associated with rock—think classical, jazz, country swing, etc. Then consider Fogerty's example of borrowing the rhythm and opening chords for his own song. Listen for elements of the music that you could borrow that would sound unique or original if used in the setting of a rock song. This kind of cross-fertilization, in which you combine elements of two distinct styles, is one sure path to innovation.

9) Explore unusual sounds with any effects pedals you own or can borrow. Hearing a strange tone from your amp often inspires a riff, and plenty of great songs have started this way. Some pedals to try include a delay, chorus, wah-wah, vibrato, octavizer, and phaser.

    No matter what the pedal, though, the key is to explore all the sounds it can produce. Try the pedals alone and in combination with each other. Use them in unusual ways. For example, if you tweak the knobs, a delay pedal can give a guitar an odd, almost metallic sound. Again, experiment. Play with the pedals like the toys they are until you find a sound you like.

10) This chapter included a section on fingerpicking, but there are countless other styles and techniques that can't be covered in the space of this book. Playing with a slide or using open tunings are just two good examples. Read books. Watch other guitarists and absorb what they know. In short, keep learning and exploring. And every time you master a technique, write a song using it. This will keep your chops fresh and ensure that you continually extend your range as a player and songwriter.

Chapter Three
The Verse and Chorus: Shaping the Heart of the Song

Any song that takes more than twenty minutes to write isn't worth writing.
— Peter Buck, quoting Sky Saxon of the Seeds

For much of its history, rock and roll has relied on very basic chord changes, which is one reason it has been dismissed by many as simple-minded music. Jazz musicians, for example, are bored by the repetitive cycle of three or four major chords that rock songwriters hammer home. Of course, some rock musicians feel the same way, and have worked diligently to expand the sonic register of the music, offering melodies and harmonies whose complexity rivals more high-brow fare. But for every artist like Yes, there's a band like the Ramones banging out a minimalist response, for every composer such as Frank Zappa, there's Nirvana offering a scorching, three-chord rejoinder.

Wherever your tastes run on this spectrum, you'll want to understand the basic harmonic structure of rock music so you know how to write the song you want to write. And in order to do that, we'll need to take a short tour through some basic musical theory.

At their most rudimentary, rock songs are built around chords corresponding to the eight notes in the traditional Western musical scale. These notes are often represented in a series of nonsense syllables, which almost every child learns: Do-Re-Me-Fa-So-La-Ti-Do. In order to see how a major scale works in terms of actual notes, let's take an example from the key of C:

Do	Re	Me	Fa	So	La	Ti	Do
C	D	E	F	G	A	B	C

On staff lines, the scale of C major looks like this:

Example 3.1: C Major Scale

The note on which the scale begins, or the tonic of the key, is C. The notes then proceed in a series of set intervals as follows:

whole step	whole step	half step	whole step	whole step	whole step	half step
^	^	^	^	^	^	^
C	D	E	F	G	A	B	C

Once you master this series of intervals, you can easily construct a major scale in any key, starting on any note. So, for example, if you want to build a G major scale, simply start on G and follow the pattern set above:

whole step	whole step	half step	whole step	whole step	whole step	half step
^	^	^	^	^	^	^
G	A	B	C	D	E	F#	G

You'll note that in order to preserve the order of intervals here, we have to add a sharp to the F note (doing so keeps the interval from E to F# a whole step, and the interval from F# to G a half step). This is, of course, where key signatures come from, and why sheet music in the key of G always includes a sharp on the F line of the staff.

Now that we have the basics of the major scale down, we can examine how this sequence helps us outline the important chords employed in any particular key. The main chord form in music is the *triad,* so-named because of its three note structure. A triad consists of a *root note*, which gives its name to the chord, and notes that, in terms of intervals, are a third and fifth above that root. To build the chords that fit well harmonically with the key of C, we simply put together a series of triads based on each step of the C major scale.

If we go on to build all seven chords based on the C scale, they will look like this:

Example 3.2: Chords in the Key of C

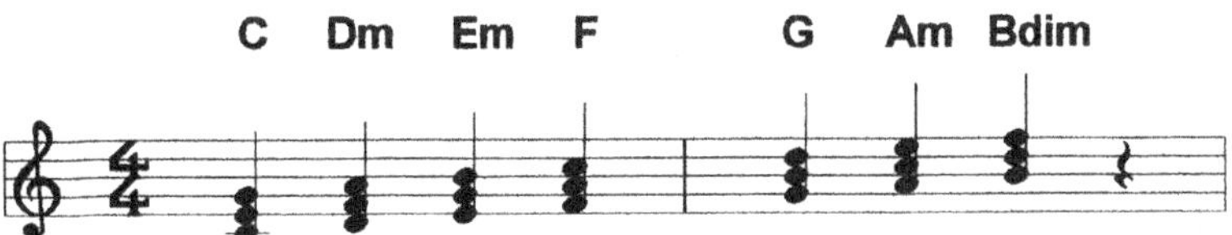

The first chord here is a simple C major: we build it by starting with the root note of C, then adding an E (a third above C in the scale), and finally a G (a fifth above C in the scale). This happens to be a major chord because of the way the intervals between the notes are spaced: we have an interval called a *major third* (comprised of 2 whole steps) between the C and E, and an interval called a *minor third* (comprised of 1½ steps) between the E and G notes.

If we reverse those intervals and have a minor third below a major third, we construct a minor chord. So in the example above, when we build a D chord using the C scale, we find that the third above D is an F (1½ steps, or a minor third interval), and a fifth above D is a A (the interval between F and A is 2 whole steps, or a major third): a minor third below a major third forms a minor chord, so we have built a D minor. And we now know that a D minor chord (rather than a D major) will sound harmonious in the key of C.

If we extend the exercise above to all the keys, we can easily identify the chords that have traditionally "belonged" in them. Here is a chart of the essential chords in major keys most commonly used by rock songwriters (note that for easy reference, musicians often refer to the chords in a key by their number in the scale, represented by a roman numeral. It's capitalized if the chord is major, and not capitalized if it's minor or diminished. For example, the IV chord in the key of C is F major, and the vi chord is A minor):

Key	I	ii	iii	IV	V	vi	Vii
C	C	dm	em	F	G	am	bdim
G	G	am	bm	C	D	em	f#dim
D	D	em	f#m	G	A	bm	c#dim
A	A	bm	c#m	D	E	f#m	g#dim
E	E	f#m	g#m	A	B	c#m	d#dim
F	F	gm	am	Bflat	F#	g#m	a#dim

To experienced musicians, of course, such chord construction is taken for granted. But if you haven't seen a chord chart laid out this way, it can look like you have found the holy grail of songwriting.

A quick scan of this chart reveals that rock songs rely heavily on the I—IV—V progression. In fact, one of the first guitar instruction books I ever worked with included a list of hundreds of songs that you could play using those three basic chords in any key. That's largely due to rock's origins in the twelve-bar blues, so-named because it is comprised of twelve measures that are repeated throughout the song. The pattern for the blues looks like this:

I (4 bars)—IV (2 bars)—I (2 bars)—V (1 bar)—IV (1 bar)—I (1 bar)—V (1 bar)

Rock and roll players took this pattern, repeated it, altered it, re-arranged it, and utterly transformed it. But those three chords, I—IV—V, still form the heart of many tunes you hear on the radio today.

Add the next most common chord, the vi (or minor six), and you can devise a list of hundreds more songs you can play. The basic pattern is reflected in the classic Everly Brothers' "All I Have to Do is Dream," in this case played in the key of E:

I—vi—IV—V

Beatle fans, of course, also recognize this as the main section of "Happiness is a Warm Gun," performed in the key of C. Armed with this arsenal of chords, and understanding their harmonic relation to one another, you should now have at least a basic sense of classic song construction. The trick, then, concerns how you put these chords together to form a song that you can justifiably call "original."

Only Connect

The first answer to the question of how you can take these established chords and create an original pattern is simple: you can't. That is, it's very difficult to create an original *sequence* of chords—and you can prove this to yourself with a bit of math. There are only so many chords, and so many possible combinations of chords. Therefore, most songs do not actually contain stunningly original chord changes. Rather, they gain their originality from other places, such as their dynamics, their tone, and their rhythm (which I'll discuss in chapter five), from their melody, and from the way they connect the chords to one another.

Let's take a fairly straightforward change, from E minor to D, and see what it would look like if you gave it a generic strumming pattern:

Example 3.3

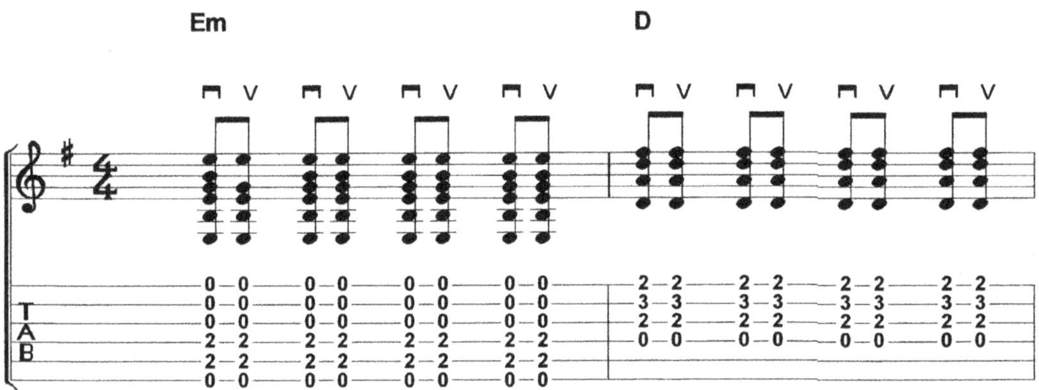

Not much here to hold your interest, not even a faint hint of a melody line. In short, there's nothing surprising to play or listen to with a chord change like this one. So what can you do to spice it up? For starters, you might think of a way to get from one chord to another that gives us a hook:

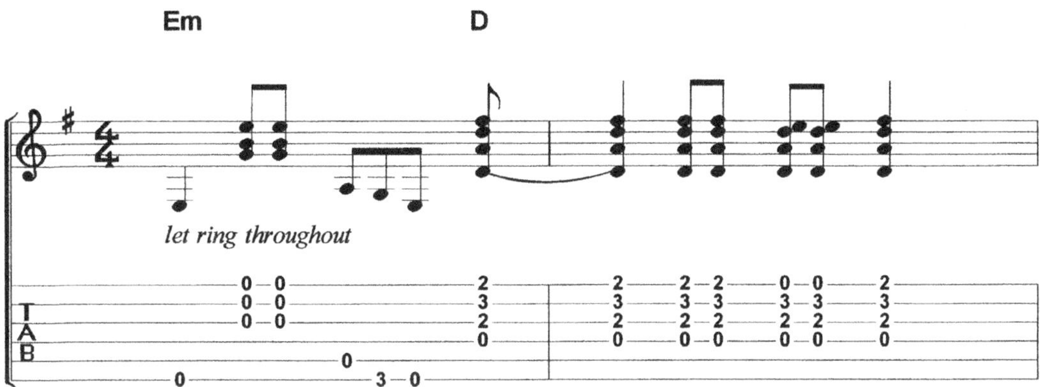

This line is reminiscent of R.E.M.'s song "The One I Love," and offers a very basic, but still compelling run. In short, the lick helps define the chord change and gives it distinction. R.E.M.'s guitarist Peter Buck has said that he considers it his main job to build bridges between chords. While not an arresting lead player (and he claims he never wanted to be, anyway), Buck consistently demonstrates his prowess as a songwriter by constructing such definitive runs.

If you begin examining the tabs presented every month in guitar magazines, you'll see just how many songs have basic, very conventional chord changes. The tunes largely follow those major chords outlined in the chart above—sometimes with a surprise thrown in, sometimes not. The real secret lies in how those chords are played: look carefully at the voicings of the chords, along with the way they're picked and how the transitions between the chords are handled.

The one clear lesson here is that very few professional musicians and songwriters play generic, strummed parts: because they often rely on fairly standard chord changes, these writers cannot afford to simply strum away on chords in an open position. Such a tactic is deadly for the originality of your songs, and the exercises at the end of this chapter offer some suggestions for getting around this problem.

Nothing New Under the Sun

Above I suggested that songwriters largely rely on well-worn chord changes because, quite simply, they have to given the limited number of chords available. And even when songwriters step outside the limitations of the traditional key structure in their search for chords (and violate the order of the chord chart above), those seemingly original changes often have a long history themselves.

For our example here, let's take a look at the chords to what ought to be a fairly simple rock song from the 1960s, the Monkee's tune "(I'm not Your) Steppin' Stone." This particular song comes with a lot of baggage: it was performed by studio musicians sitting in for a pre-fabricated band put together to make money on a t.v. show loosely based on Beatles' films. We shouldn't expect much from the songs, right? Here's a sequence of chords similar to those that carry the verse to the song: all the chords are in the open position, and should be played firmly on each beat.

E—E G—G A—A C—C

If you take these simple major chords and go back to the chord chart above, you'll notice something interesting: the chords don't fit. G major and C major don't work in the key of E as it's laid out. Nor can you smash all four chords into any other key. They just do not sit well together in a traditional key structure. There are two points worth noting here: 1) "Steppin' Stone" was written by Tommy Boyce and Bobby Hart, master pop songwriters who were far more crafty than we might initially suppose, and 2) even by the mid-1960s, rock songs had gone well beyond the 1950s three or four chord formula.

All well and good, you say, but how does this relate to contemporary songs? Let's take a look at a chord progression similar to the one that opens Nirvana's "Rape Me." The title alone tells us that we've moved quite a ways from the Monkees, and the music certainly sounds different. In this example, the A and E chords should be played open, and the C and G played as barre chords. Again, each chord gets one beat of in the riff. (Keep in mind that in Cobain's song, all the guitar strings are tuned down 1/2 step.)

A—A C—C E—E G—G

Now compare the chords here to those employed in the riff above: if you listen to "Steppin' Stone" and "Rape Me," you'll hear a slightly different rhythm, but the same four chords and virtually the same chord sequence—except that Kurt Cobain starts the progression on the A rather than the E chord. And again, neither "Steppin' Stone" nor "Rape Me" fits neatly into our chord chart above.

The example of Nirvana's "Rape Me" as a transformation of The Monkee's song might strike you as bizarre coincidence. So let's examine another series of chord changes that have a long history in rock. A three-chord riff, this one's similar to the opening of the Kink's song "All Day and All of the Night," ultimately covered by Van Halen and countless other bands. The chords should be played on the low E and A strings, and include only the root and fifth notes:

F—G   G—F F—Bflat—Bflat—G

In the Kink's song, these simple, raunchy two-note chords underpin a melody that closely follows the chord progression.

The next example is similar to the Doors' song "Hello, I Love You," which offers a chord progression like this one (the chords should all be barred):

A—G—C—A

If you listen to the Doors' song, you'll hear a slightly different rhythm from "All Day and All of the Night" and a bit more complex musical backing, with the addition of the keyboard and a clever guitar lick that sends us back to the beginning. But if you examine the chord changes, you'll see the very same pattern underlying them(I-Flat VII-Flat III-I) simply in a different key. And if you focus on the melody, you'll quickly find that it does pretty much what the "All Day and All of the Night" did—the tune closely mirrors those chord changes.

The final example comes from the late 1970s and the birth of punk. Here's a selection that resembles the opening of the Sex Pistols' "Submission." Again, the chords are all barred, and the rhythm offers a pumping bass played on the root and fifth notes of the chord, punctuated with a slash across the high strings on every off beat.

B—A—D—B

Ok—you get the idea. These chord changes, too, have been hashed over pretty well in rock music. Once again we have the same sequence of chords (though in a different key), a melody closely following the chords, and a strong rhythm driving the tune. What may be a little surprising is that bands as different as the Doors and the Sex Pistols use such similar tactics. Yes, the Sex Pistols mark a return to rudimentary sound based on relatively simple chord shapes, and they use a blazing distortion that rivals the raunchiness of "All Day and All of the Night," but the song structure remains virtually unchanged.

What have we discovered in our short tour through rock history? Simply that most chord changes to most songs have been done before. If you think just about recorded music in the past hundred years, and include pop tunes, jazz standards, country and western numbers, and rock songs, imagine how many times the basic chord changes in a major key have been recycled.

At first this thought seems daunting: with such a history of music behind you, how on earth could you ever come up with something original? But this thought also contains an element of freedom. Consider how original the Sex Pistols and Nirvana are deemed to be by both fans and rock critics—they are bands that, without exaggeration, changed the direction of rock music. And they both wrote songs based on progressions that are hardly original. The lesson should be to put far less pressure on yourself as a writer to come up with a chord change that nobody has thought of before. What makes a song original has as much to do with the sound of the band as it does with the chord changes: listen to "Steppin' Stone" and "Rape Me" back to back and you'll find that the chords are certainly the least of what distinguishes them from each other.

So What's New?

I've made a strong case for the lack of originality in rock songwriting, at least in terms of the chord progressions—and I did so for one reason: to help you see that there's nothing wrong with recycling those chords. Everybody does it, and you should be able to write a song easily either within or outside the traditional key structure without worrying too much about finding a completely original chord sequence.

I purposely overstated the case, however, because there clearly are ways to achieve an element of surprise through your chords, and I want to outline a couple of those methods below.

Finding The Lost Chord

Even if you are composing a song with a fairly conventional chord progression, you can easily inject originality into it by employing an unusual or unexpected chord. By unusual I mean several things:

- chords played with non-traditional voicings
- extended chords
- "unusual chords" that simply don't appear often in rock songs

For a discussion of voicings, see chapter five on arranging your material, and for the use of extended chords, see chapter two on writing the intro. Here I want to focus on the use of quirky chords that, by themselves, can lend your song distinction. One master of this is Neil Young, who from the beginning of his career explored startling alternatives to the usual fare of open chords in expected positions.

Let's take as an example Neil Young's "Sugar Mountain" to see how you can effectively employ some riveting chords. Tuned down one full step, the guitar part in the verse of Young's song relies on a standard open G chord that alternates with a peculiar F chord—an F (add G) to be exact. The chord shape looks like this:

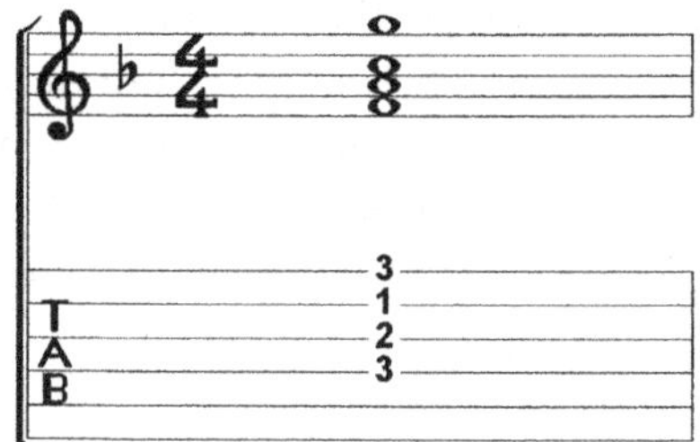

Young creates a rich harmonic field that reinforces the song's nostalgic tone simply by planting a finger on that sixth string and adding the G note to the F chord (here I'm referring to the fingering of these chords, not the actual tonality with the guitar tuned down a step). After moving through the chorus, Young adds a transition back to the verse that begins with another startling chord:

Example 3.6

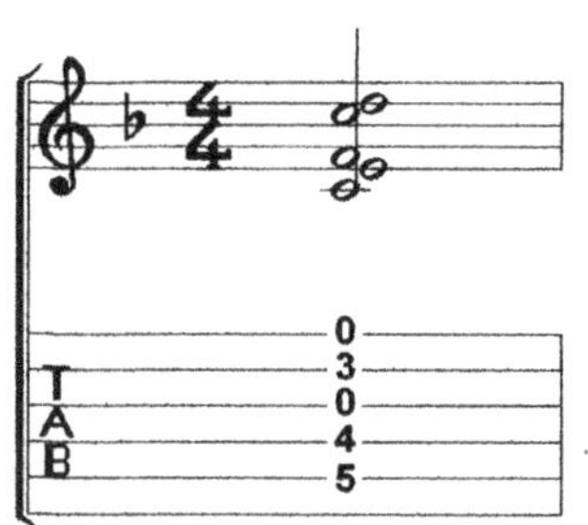

Moving the open C chord form up the neck two frets and allowing the notes to ring, he offers an evocative harmony that perfectly resonates with the lyrics.

Why are such chords so effective? Obviously because the chords grab your attention—your rock and roll ear probably isn't used to hearing that kind of tonal complexity. These chords work their magic because of their harmonic range: even a slight variation in a standard chord can breed radical new melodic possibilities. And that's what you're looking for when writing an original song.

Exploring New Intervals

Just as "Steppin' Stone" employed chords outside the standard key signature to create a distinctive progression, so many recent bands are finding creative ways to expand even further outside the traditional chord chart. For example, one specific method of doing this involves the use of half-step intervals. A well known example of this tactic occurs in the opening to the Green Day tune "Basket Case." This riff begins with a very common I—V change, moving from the D to the A chord. Then the song offers up its surprising twists. Play this section using the familiar root-fifth chord shapes:

$$B - F\# - G - D - A$$

Ultimately, all the chords here belong to the key of D (as we can see in the chart above). In other words, it would not be surprising to find a song from fifty years ago that contained these chords—what makes the song stand out is the way they are deployed.

In the key of D, the B chord should be a minor, but here its tonality remains ambiguous because it only contains the root and the fifth note. The riff then moves to F#, which again should be a minor, and again remains undefined. Perhaps the most surprising move, though, is the abrupt half-step shift from the F# to the G chord, with little attempt to make this a smooth transition. Along with the pumping, eighth-note rhythm, the jagged quality of the progression gives the song its punkish tinge.

The lesson from Green Day—which they learned from the Ramones and the Sex Pistols, of course—is that half-step intervals and abrupt shifts signal an attitude, one that defies the musical tradition of seamless chord changes and flowing transitions. One way to make your song original, then, is to further explore such unusual movement between chords.

It's Time for the Chorus: Everybody Sing

This chapter has been devoted to the construction of chord progressions—ones that are original in themselves or that signal their originality in the transitions between chords. I want to conclude with a brief discussion of what happens in a rock song when we move to the chorus.

First, consider a few of the qualities of a song's chorus: almost always higher in the singer's vocal range than the verse, the melody is also generally stronger, shorter and more repetitive—and the chord changes have to support this movement.

As with all of the supposed "rules" for songwriting, of course, we can instantly find songs that violate them. The simplest form of chorus in rock and roll is, in fact, no chorus. That is, the song merely repeats the chords of the verse, but with a new melody perhaps laid over a variation on the rhythm. The most famous, poorly-covered, and by now hopelessly clichéd version of this arrangement occurs in the Kingsmen's classic "Louie, Louie." Too bad the song has been done to death by musical hacks—because it does have radical features, including one of the wildest guitar solos on record. But generally speaking, you can bang out this song with three chords (I—IV—V) in any key, and almost everyone will recognize it.

Most songs, however, will introduce a new chord sequence for the chorus to signal a shift in the song's movement and call attention to the heightened emotion. As in the verse, you can employ chords in the traditional key structure, or be more adventurous in exploring other sonic possibilities.

In short, for the chorus in most of your songs, you'll probably want to compose a chord progression that is either a subtle or significant deviation from the verse. You can make the chorus original through methods similar to those discussed above: 1) pay attention to the transitions between the chords, including guitar fills or even heavy licks to announce the arrival of this new section of the song; 2) consider changing your tone, rhythm, or playing style to underscore the importance of shifting musical gears for the chorus; and 3) experiment with surprising chords—ones that fall outside the key structure or ones that include unusual extensions—to give you new melodic possibilities.

Keep in mind that choruses are typically brief and repetitive: that design ensures that they are memorable and people can sing along with them. If a part to a song gets stuck in your head, it's usually either the intro guitar line or the chorus—and that's why those two sections of the tune deserve the most detailed attention as you compose.

Exercises

1) Try writing a song using only one or, at most, two chords. Focus at first on finding a rhythm that you think will be compelling enough to hold the listener's attention. In working within such harmonic restrictions, you will most likely find that the song's success largely depends on the melody and its variations. In this sense, the tune might well resemble Indian classical music, with its drone-like quality and intricate web of improvisations. Be patient with this exercise—it proves rewarding in the way it forces you to pay attention to rhythm, melody, and the overall style of the song, rather than hanging onto chord changes to move the tune forward.

2) Write a song in which you consciously shift the dynamics as you transition from the verse to the chorus. One version of this is to move from a soft verse to a loud chorus, a la the Pixies or Nirvana. But also think about inverting this pattern: what would it sound like to go from a loud verse to a soft chorus?

3) Consider writing a song that goes against your basic musical instincts: if you generally are drawn to loud and fast songs, try consciously writing one slow and sparse. On the other hand, if your tunes are ponderous and downbeat, pick up the tempo and crank up the volume.

4) As you compose the parts to a song, consciously vary the style of your playing as you make the transition from verse to chorus. Try finger-picking the verse and strumming the chorus, for example. As you experiment, note how challenging it is to devise such a shift, and how much complexity it adds to your music when done successfully. This exercise is worth repeated effort.

5) Consider the rhythm of your playing as you go from verse to chorus, and try to introduce a variation in it. You'll probably find that such a change is a real musical challenge. But as you experiment with it, you'll discover that the mood or feeling of the song immediately shifts as you change the rhythm. Explore how such a change can add to the musical and emotional complexity of your tune.

6) Pick up a book of sheet music from the library. It's especially useful for this exercise if its from an artist or in a style that you are not familiar with, so if you don't like country or jazz, for example, you might start there. Then randomly pick some songs and play the chords in reverse order. Listen to see if there's a chord change that catches your ear. Of course, feel free to modify the chord sequence or alter the chords as you see fit. Then write a song based on these changes.

7) Keep in mind that a song's originality often comes from the sound of the band and how the chords are actually played (strummed, finger-picked, etc.). Pick up a songbook or a recent guitar magazine and look solely at the chords to a particular song, especially a tune that you're familiar with. Now consciously try to play these chords in a different style from the song you're examining—if they're finger-picked, strum them; if they're played quickly, play them slowly; if they're played with distortion, play them clean on an acoustic. This exercise may not lead you to your own song, but it should demonstrate how the same chord sequence can lead to radically different finished tunes.

8) Get a book of guitar chords and flip through it until you find a chord you've never played before or one that's played in a position you have not mastered. Experiment with other chords leading up to and away from this chord, then write a song based on these changes.

9) Play chords with odd intervals. Rock guitarists have long favored using the root and fifth of a chord (as in some of the examples above). So consider what it would sound like to employ the root and third or the root and minor third instead. Keep your mind open and play as many different intervals as possible, with an ear toward

what sounds new to you. Consider how you could use these intervals as the basis for a chord progression.

10) Try writing a song that employs a half-step interval. You can make this shift sound very jarring, if that fits the style of the song you're working on, which is why it may work best in a punk or alternative tune. A bigger challenge might be to make the interval jump fit seamlessly into a quieter song.

11) Compose a chord sequence that deliberately falls outside the chord chart outlined in this chapter. You might start by picking two chords from a key and then try to work in a chord or two from another, related key. For example, begin with two chords from the key of C, and then work in a chord or two from the key of G or F.

12) If you really want to bend your mind and tax your ingenuity, try this: write the names of eight or ten chords from the chord chart on individual slips of paper, then draw three or four of them randomly from a hat. Now work on hooking them together in a sequence so they sound like they belong beside each other. Remember, random connections often inspire creativity!

Chapter Four
The Solo: Writing with Style, Playing with Flair

It's been very important throughout my career that I've met all the guys I copied, because at each stage they've said, "Don't play like me, play like you."
— Eric Clapton

Many rock song rely on a simple riff-verse-chorus format and repeat the parts for two minutes of pure pop joy. But even in the earliest days of rock and roll, and even within the constraints of a two-minute single, songwriters generally had the sense that the tune needed a break or slight shift in direction to keep the listener's attention. That's where the solo comes in. At its best, the musical solo breaks the established pattern of the music and reinforces the theme by developing and adding complexity to it.

The guitar solo has a mythic status in rock and roll. It's why most guitar players started playing, if they tell the truth. It's your time in the spotlight, when you can express yourself with unfiltered electric joy—especially if it sounds fuzzy and loud. Unless you're a singer, the only time you get undivided attention occurs when you step out from the shadows and start performing your six-string soliloquy.

Because the solo carries such emotional weight for a guitarist, it's often difficult to think clearly about it. When you hear a great solo, you're probably tempted to ask, "How on earth did he play that?" Indeed, the best solos have a mystical air that reinforces certain stereotypes about creativity. To play a moving solo you must be under the spell of inspiration, using a gift bestowed upon you by a higher power. Such magical thinking surely explains the 1960's buttons that proclaimed, "Clapton is God."

Inspiration, spontaneity, and improvisation, of course, remain central to the art of performing music, and some of the most skilled guitarists in rock have relied on them. But for every story of Clapton closing his eyes and trusting god to lead his fingers on, there's another tale—for example, Clapton taking a year off to woodshed. That's right, a year off dedicated solely to refining his skills and honing his craft. The plain truth is that unless you have an immense, fully-developed talent, achieved through much patient, daily practice, you simply don't have much chance of grabbing your axe and letting loose with a remarkably original solo. More likely, you'll wind up repeating yourself, falling into the basic patterns and positions that you always use, and generally meandering through clichéd licks that everybody knows. Such playing does not add to the originality of your song – in fact, most solos played by amateurs sound distinctly disconnected from the rest of the song.

So if you want to be an improvisational genius, the road is clearly marked for you. You know that you have to put in years of practice, steadily jamming, mastering the nuances of scales, and picking up tips from every available source as you proceed on the journey. Actually, if you're a serious guitar player, you should be doing those things anyway. But here I want to make a case for a different approach, one that can have you playing more inventive, original solos much sooner.

How do you walk down the road less traveled with your solo? The short answer is that you need to plan the trip. It sounds obvious, but you can go out any night of the week and watch mediocre players noodle their way through guitar breaks as if it's the first time they've every heard the tune. In contrast, if you spend time outlining where you want to go and what you want to achieve, you can produce consistently inventive, attention-grabbing parts that help define your song.

Play a Melody

Listen to a Ramones record. Hear any solos? Punk rock in part came about in part because of the pompous, bloated solos that littered songs of the late-1960s and early 1970s. By this point in music history, the very idea of a guitar solo was in danger of becoming a cliché. The punk revolution occurred because many guitar players harbor the notion that they need to play loud and fast—very fast—or they're not really playing guitar. In this school of thought, rhythm guitar doesn't exist; the motto seems to be, "Play lead guitar or die." You know you're hearing this kind of guitarist when the "solo" quickly degenerates into a string of pointless pyrotechnics, like the following riff:

Example 4.1

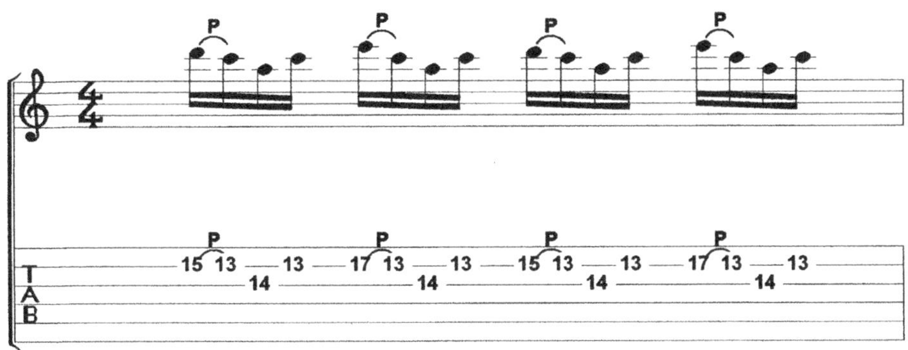

Now such licks aren't bad in themselves (as I'll argue below), and the first guitarists who discovered them were true innovators. Of course there's nothing inherently wrong with playing like a speed demon: the problem occurs when you substitute style for substance, flash for finesse. Someone once remarked that the true test for a guitar solo was whether or not you could hum it. In other words, when you play a solo, are you sticking together a bunch of tired old riffs, or are you creating something as musically distinct and important as the melody?

Guitarists often fall short of an original style because they generally learn to play solos based on scales, and one of the most common is the pentatonic. As with the standard I—IV—V chord changes, the pentatonic scale arose through rock's debt to blues music. This scale—named for its 5 steps—includes non-offensive notes that can be played over any of the basic chords in a key, but they sound particularly good when set against the standard I—IV—V change. Here's the pentatonic scale in the key of C:

Example 4.2

Dropping the 4th and the 7th notes of the major scale, the pentatonic has a fairly evident virtue: you can play it for hours over all sorts of chord changes, and it will sound basically fine—that is, you won't be in danger of hitting any offensive notes, and you can bend and slide, hammer-on and pull-off to your heart's content. But that's also the problem.

Solos built on this scale risk becoming generic because they contain no surprises, no twists or turns, and no real way of signaling a larger structure. In short, a pentatonic solo can quickly lapse into blandness, like unsalted food: you're got a lumpy, misshapen mess on your plate, and nobody will be asking for seconds. One remedy is obvious. To avoid the same intervals, bends, and beaten dead licks, you need to master other, more complex scales, and play them over many chord changes as you learn their effects.

35

But again, a quicker and more interesting route to originality exists. If you begin to play actual melodies on your guitar, you'll suddenly see how songwriters work outside the standard scales and patterns employed by novices. One clear example of such playing occurs in the solo to Eric Clapton's "Bell Bottom Blues," from the album *Layla and Other Love Songs*. Here are the first measures of a phrase in this style:

Example 4.3

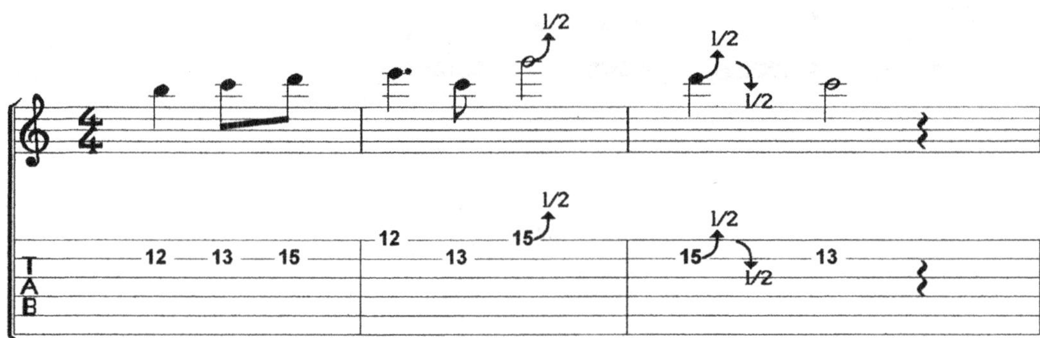

The opening notes mirror the melody of the song, letting the guitar say something that the singer can't say alone, as though Clapton here translates the emotion of the lyric into purely musical terms. Note how simply stated and evocative this phrasing is—and how different it is from the wailing nonsense you hear in many a guitar break.

For another version of this technique, listen to the solo on the Beatles' "Nowhere Man." George Harrison and John Lennon played this part in unison on their Stratocasters with the treble knobs turned up as far as they would go, and the bass knobs turned down. Aside from the wonderful ringing tone, the guitar part is distinguished because it actually inverts the melody of the song. In other words, when the melody of the song goes higher, the guitar part goes lower, and vice versa. Look at the opening measures of this solo and compare them with the melody:

Example 4.4

If you aspire to this level of inventiveness in your own songs, start by picking out the melodies on your guitar. Along with being excellent ear training, such an exercise immediately tells you how interesting your melody is. But it can also help you fashion a more compelling lead part. In your solo, of course, you don't need to mindlessly repeat the tune, but feel free to take the general pattern of notes or a few of the striking intervals and employ them as a foundation to build upon. That way, what you play won't sound like a disconnected jam, but will develop into an integral part of the tune itself.

Tell a Story

Aside from devising a guitar line that reflects the melody, you're always free to invent a new melody that complements your song (some rock and jazz guitarists actually sing along as they play). It's helpful when laying out such a part to think of what you're doing as telling part of the story of the song, and as in any narrative, the solo should have a beginning, middle, and end. The opening will catch the listener's attention and lay down a melodic premise that the rest of the guitar break will build upon. As the solo develops, you'll want to shift the dynamics and probably move to a higher register so that you create a sense of drama and tension in your playing. At its conclusion, the solo should clearly signal the end of the instrumental break and bring some resolution to the tension that has built up.

One catchy version of this narrative tactic can be heard on the Knack's song "My Sharona." Yes, the band has gotten a bad rap from critics who think the music hasn't aged very well. But the masterful playing on this track deserves attention. In fact, it's worth studying for the compelling way the band shifts to the solo section alone. First, the song comes to a halt, leaving the rhythm guitar to strum a basic I—V—IV—V change in the key of C. Then the band kicks back in with the lead guitar, all playing in a different key from the preceding verses and on top of a different, looser rhythm. Here's a guitar riff similar to the opening of that solo:

Example 4.5

With a deft touch, including some sweet slides, bends, and hammer-ons, lead guitarist Berton Averre offers a new melody here, distinct from the song's verse and chorus but just as sing-able. This opening helps launch an extended solo that finally erupts into a crescendo of wild riffs, not unlike example 4.1 above. Such licks make sense here because they don't arrive out of nowhere; they've been set up the preceding melodic section, and they occur as the climax to the increasing tension of the solo. In this example, riffs that seem over-done take on a new life—when they are employed in the right context and as the culmination of the "story" in the solo.

Finally, in "My Sharona," Averre concludes the solo by mimicking the rhythm of the chord changes with a series of strong bends. Such an ending helps release the tension built up in those dazzling high runs, and paves the way for the transition back to the verse. Here's an original riff in the style of Averre's guitar line:

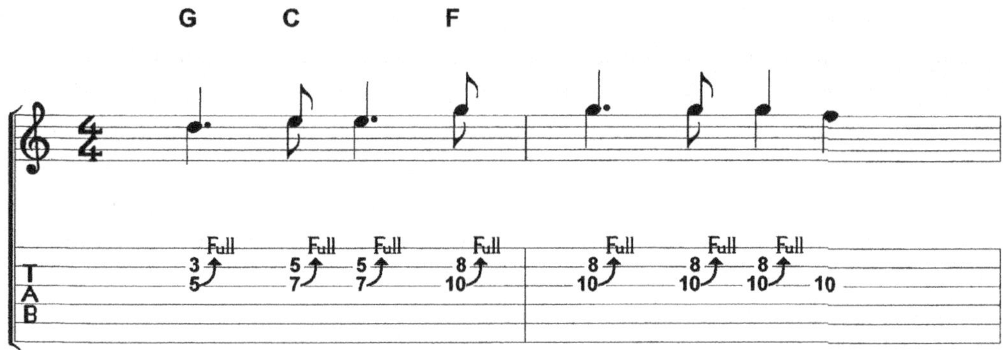

Note that the rhythm here reflects that of the very beginning of the solo, and so ties the whole package together. In short, it's clear Averre knew what he was doing: he states a theme, develops and amplifies it, and then reiterates it at the end. Although this is an elaborate and highly complicated version of the guitar solo as narrative, the basic structure works well for solos of any length. The next time you hear a guitar solo, listen to how closely it follows this pattern of development.

Be a Guitar Anti-Hero

One certain way to achieve originality, or at least notoriety, is to become an iconoclast. That is, every time you hear a piece of advice, turn it on its head. Every time you notice a musical pattern being used, thwart it. In short, find out what everyone else is saying or doing, and negate it. And so it is with guitar solos. If you can't stand the thought of melodic guitar lines, then by all means, produce anti-melodies. If you don't want to tell a story with your solo, then create ruptured, angular guitar lines that defy development.

You can produce playing of this sort by composing lines that no one would (or could) ever actually sing. Play incredibly fast, use wild jumps in notes that a singer could not reproduce, or simply employ weird riffs that do not sound sing-able: any one of these will make your guitar line stand out. As one example, here's a great little riff similar to that found in the Talking Heads' song "Television Man":

Example 4.7

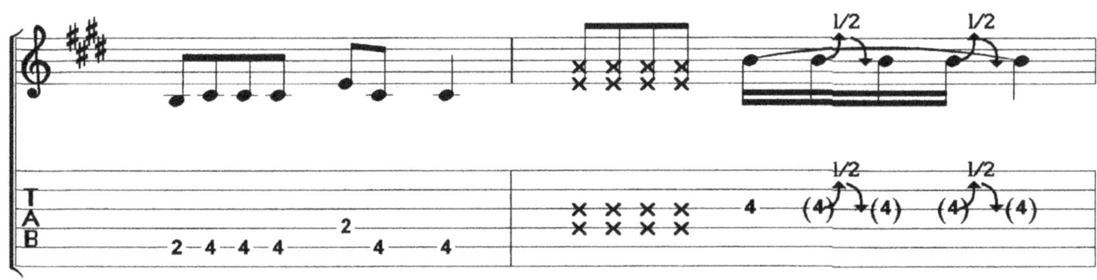

Not a solo in the conventional sense, this part clearly shows the power of violating the melodic order of the song. Jerry Harrison's fractured, staccato playing achieves its effect by denying smooth transitions and jabbing at the listener with the notes, then throwing in some manic bends for good measure. To be fair, this riff does in fact slightly echo the melody of the sing-along part in the bridge, but Harrison performs the part in a style that perfectly exemplifies the anti-melodic tendency I'm advocating here.

Another way to challenge the melody-driven solo is simply to refuse to change notes. That's right—produce a one-note solo. You could sing it, of course, but why on earth would you want to? A master of such radical abandon in his electric guitar playing, Neil Young savages the idea of a guitar solo pretty completely in his raucous "Cinnamon Girl." The solo offers a riff similar to the following:

Example 4.8

Tune high and low E down one full step: D-A-D-G-B-D

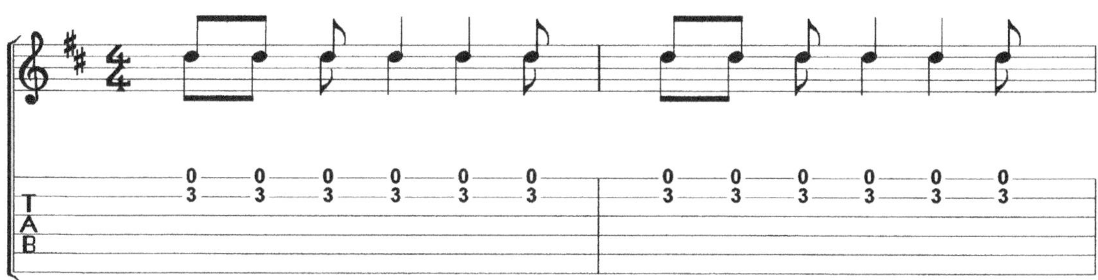

Note that while the melody is unchanging, the part does have harmonic interest, mainly because he plays the single note over a series of shifting chords (D—Am7sus4—Csus2—G). You can try multiple versions of such a solo—in the right song—to see what effects you might achieve.

Finally, there's a tactic that to my ears has not been fully exploited in rock music: the chord solo. Instead of using single, wailing riffs based in the blues, consider how you could incorporate two- or three-note chords in your solo. Examples of such an approach generally occur in the work of guitarists who are not considered virtuosos. The earliest one in rock, of course, is Buddy Holly (listen to the break on "Peggy Sue"). But other bands, including the Who, the Replacements, and R.E.M. have employed this compelling approach (listen to the Replacements' "I Will Dare," for example).

Here's an example of a chord solo based on the changes to the Who's tune "Can't Explain." The first two measures contain full chords, and the final two show how they can easily be broken down to suggest melody:

Example 4.9

In the Who's version, Pete Townshend fractures these chords in other ways, and plays an off-kilter rhythm that suggests an immense, wild energy. Again, Townshend is not known as phenomenal soloist in the blues tradition, but his cagey exploitation of harmonies and chord-based riffs marks him as an extraordinarily original player.

When you're composing a solo for one of your songs, consider the remarkable variety of approaches available to you. Each one can be bent or twisted or tweaked so that it fits your individual style of playing and blends seamlessly into your song. Above all, don't settle for a mediocre solo in which you meander around a tired scale. Think instead of the melody, the momentum, the tone, and the overall story you're telling through your playing.

Exercises

1) Play melodies on your guitar. It's best if you pick them out by ear, but you can start by reading any sheet music. This is a classic method of ear training because it forces you to practice hearing intervals. It works extremely well for developing your abilities as a soloist because it helps break those hackneyed scale patterns.

2) Plot out the melody to one of your songs on your guitar. Now play that tune in a few different positions on the guitar (and in different octaves), adding harmony notes or filler runs as you see fit. Consider how you might use this as the basis for a solo. It might help here to listen to some classic instrumental music—anything by Chet Atkins or Wes Montgomery, for example. You'll hear how beautifully a simple tune can be played when performed by a master.

3) Take a chord sequence you're working on for the verse to the song and begin searching for a new chord (i.e., one you haven't yet used in the song) to introduce the solo or bridge. Don't limit your imagination, but seek out unusual chords and voicings. Here again, it might be effective to violate the chord chart from chapter three: if you're working in the key of C, shift to a chord from the key of G or F to see what harmonic possibilities such a change invites.

4) One evocative method for opening the solo or bridge is to vary the kind of chord you play: in other words, songwriters often shift the mood of a tune by employing a minor chord, especially if the verse heavily relies on major chords. Of course, you can experiment with this tactic by considering extended chords, including seventh, ninth, or thirteenth chords, or any other creative variation of a traditional triad.

5) When writing a solo or bridge for a song, try introducing a new rhythm as well. This change of pace will add a new dimension to your tune, giving it a more complex emotional resonance that might go well with the new chords you use to introduce this section of the song.

6) After you have composed a verse and chorus to a song, try completely changing the key when you move to the bridge or solo: that is, if you're working in the key of C, don't just add a chord from the key of G, but actually move to the key of G. This can easily be done by making the transition point a chord that is shared by both keys. So you can move from C to G by using a G chord, or from C to F using the F chord, etc. Again, experiment, and note that the further you move from your home key the harder the transition will be—that's what makes this exercise a rewarding challenge.

7) Invent a break to introduce the bridge or solo. The song could come to a complete halt, or the drums might drop out, or everything but the drums might drop out. But find some significant way to stop and signal that the song is changing directions. A short guitar lick here could be effective—you might even try doubling it an octave higher of lower.

8) For a solo to one on your songs, completely change the rhythm, don't just vary it slightly. If done well, the part should sound almost as though you're moving to another song, yet still retain some connection to the rest

of the work. This tactic succeeds best when it's used at the end of a song for an extended solo or a jam, though with enough ingenuity you could insert it effectively in the middle of a tune. Strangely enough, such a move actually aligns your composition with classical music, which is far more bold in shifting rhythm, tempo, and tonality than most rock music.

9) Design a short solo to one of your songs using four or five notes at most. Such a restriction will force you to be creative in choosing the notes and intervals. It also demonstrates that many times a song doesn't need a full-blown, over-the-top guitar solo. In other words, if you push yourself you can find concise ways to make your song more musical. Finally, this exercise is useful because it pushes you to write a distinct part for the guitar (see chapter five for a full discussion of the importance of arrangements).

10) Try viewing one of your solos as a story. Take it apart and look at it as though it had three distinct sections. What do you do at the beginning that is attention-grabbing and that sets out your melodic approach to the solo as a whole? In the middle section, how do you ratchet up the tension: do you play faster, or higher, or introduce new notes and intervals that add a musical twist? Finally, how do you wrap it all up and signal your return to the song? What about it tells the listener that it's over?

11) When composing a solo for a song, consider the tonal range of your playing. That is, ask yourself whether you play the solo all in one position and in essentially one octave. If so, brainstorm for a way to include some very low notes and some much higher ones as you build to the climax of the part. Doing so not only adds excitement to your playing, but it also will help you build working knowledge of the full length of the fretboard.

12) Instead of composing a standard single-note solo based on the blues, try these various restrictions as you prepare to take a lead: a) include several chords as well as single notes in your part; b) compose a solo that includes no bends, slides, pull-offs, or hammer-ons; c) sing the solo as you play it.

13) Experiment with unusual tones for the solo to one of your songs. If you invariably stomp on the distortion pedal to produce a white-noise wall of sound, think clean. Also, consider your full range of options: what would your song sound like with an acoustic guitar solo—or even a classical guitar solo? Finally, with so many great digital effects available, you can spend days looking for an arresting tone that sounds far different from anything you've used before.

14) Ok, for all the discussion of planning, don't try to deny any element of spontaneity in your playing. Sometimes it is helpful to let 'er rip. When you've got a song in fairly solid shape except for the guitar solo— leave it a blank space. Then when your band plays the tune (or when you go to record the guitar part), play whatever comes to mind with only one restriction: make it interesting. You might not produce a perfect, completed solo, but you may well find some good ideas that you can use as you put the finished part together. (That's one of several reasons why it's a good idea to tape the rehearsal of your songs).

Chapter Five
The Arrangement: Putting it All Together for the Band

Music, in performance, is a type of sculpture. The air in the performance is sculpted into something.

— Frank Zappa

So you've got your intro honed to perfection, you've hammered out the chords for the verse, you've made the chorus in all its sing-along glory stand out from the rest of the song, and you're kicking around ideas for a mind-bending solo. Get the band together and plug in! This should be the easy part. Unfortunately, though, it's where the problems set in for many aspiring songwriters. They wind up with music that falls far short of what they imagined when they were composing it. That's because too many writers think so long and so hard about the structure of the song that they ignore the last crucial piece of the puzzle: arranging the song for performance.

Why does the arrangement get short shrift? It's partly because nothing in rock gets written down. If you were writing classical music, putting together a score would force you as you composed to make a hundred decisions about who plays what, how quickly, and how loudly, and it would all be there in black and white for the musicians to read as they play. Neglecting the arrangement also is due to the fact that you have to work things out with other musicians – and bless them all, each one probably has many ideas about how the song should sound. I mean, really, shouldn't the bass part be a bit more complex than what you imagined? And why shouldn't there be a five-minute drum solo?

Of course, I am overstating the case here: I don't mean to dismiss the contributions of other musicians to your material. They can offer ideas that turn a mediocre song into a great tune. For example, the singer in my band once suggested that one of our tunes come to a complete stop for a short guitar break before the bridge: it made the song. My point is that these ideas can help refine or add a new dimension to your song, and you should solicit that kind of input. But if you show up to rehearsal with an ill-defined composition to start with, you're likely to be disappointed when you hear the band play it.

The Whole is the Sum of the Parts

When arranging a piece for your band, the key point to keep in mind can be summed up in one short phrase: think in parts. How is this different than the way a song typically gets presented to a band? When you present new material, you most likely haul out your guitar and strum through the chord changes while singing it. You might have a few ideas for an intro or for a guitar break, but most of the time, the other musicians are left on their own to work out their parts individually. If you've got a great band, this method of arranging can work just fine. Then it simply takes some extensive practice to work out the rough edges of the song.

Too often, though, your band-mates won't have a clear image of the song you're trying to write if you present it in such a vague way. Take an example from Pete Townshend and the Who. Townshend has released two full records worth of demos, called *Scoop* and *Another Scoop,* that he made to present to his band. These versions of the songs are stunning in how intricately arranged they were *before* the band ever heard them. Keep in mind that Townshend could rely on John Entwistle on bass and Keith Moon on drums! Yet he still carefully set out the parts that they could then fill in or modify. The point is that when Townshend writes a song, he writes the whole song, and he has very clear ideas about how the finished product will be performed.

Even if you're unfamiliar with how to play bass or drums, you can still apply Townshend's lesson to the guitar parts for your material. In short, you need to move beyond thinking of songs as chord changes with a melody. This means that if you choose to have a guitar strumming open chords or standard barre chords, it has to be just that—a choice, not a default assumption that you need a guitar playing such a part. The problem of generic guitar (or what many call "camp-fire guitar") raises its head most noticeably in bands with two guitarists. It's difficult enough to compose an intriguing part for yourself. But if you don't think of a part for the other player as well, or encourage him to come up with his own, you're going to have one dull song on your hands.

To avoid such blandness, keep one simple idea in mind as you approach your songs: use as few instruments as you need to perform them well. Just because you have two guitar players does not mean that any particular song needs two guitars on it. The same goes for keyboards, bass guitar, drums, and every other instrument. Your attitude should be that unless they have well-defined parts to play, the other musicians should sit out. That will force your hand as arranger, and make the parts you devise crucial to the success of the song.

Think Like an Arranger

How should you think about coming up with parts for a guitar? Here's a little test for you. Before looking at the tab below, stop, pick up your guitar, and play A and E major chords in as many different positions as you possibly can, all the way up the fretboard.

Example 5.1

A Major Chords

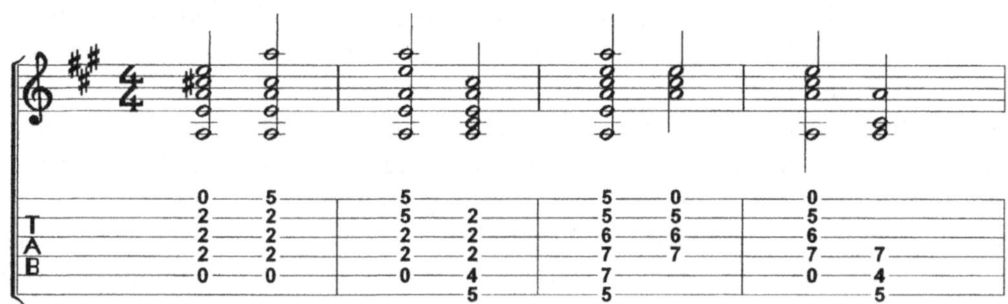

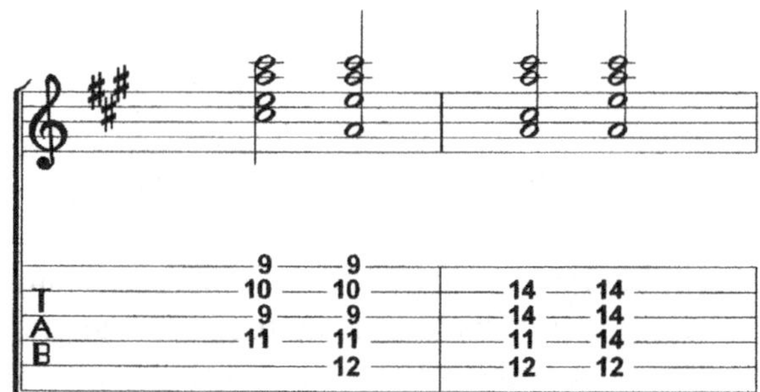

E Major Chords

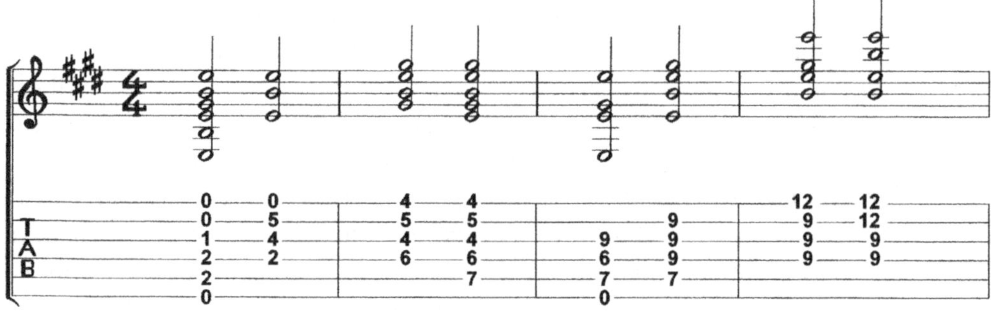

In the above examples, I tried to eliminate variations on the same chord shape (that is, simply adding an additional note to a particular chord shape)—and I still came up with twelve possible ways to play each one. Consider that example when you're arranging a part: push yourself to try new voicings, ones that you don't typically play, and see if they inspire you to detail a distinctive part for you song.

A great way to gain familiarity with arrangements is to listen to classic examples with an ear for the parts. One fantastic record to study is Lucinda Williams' *Car Wheels on a Gravel Road*. Each song has multiple guitar parts, interwoven and layered into a stunning tapestry, and every time you listen to it you'll hear something new. Note that many times the guitar parts here are not extraordinarily difficult. To take one example from the bag of tricks on this record, let's look at a straightforward set of chord changes, all played in the open position, reminiscent of the song "Right in Time":

Example 5. 2

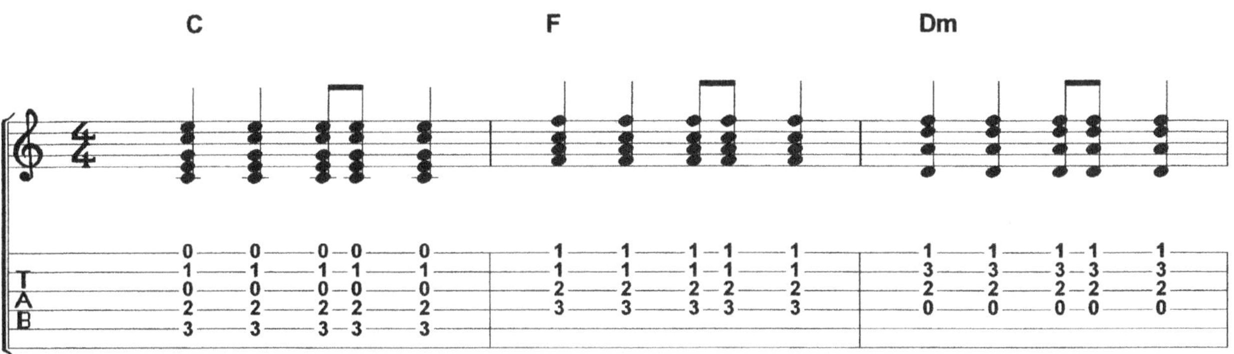

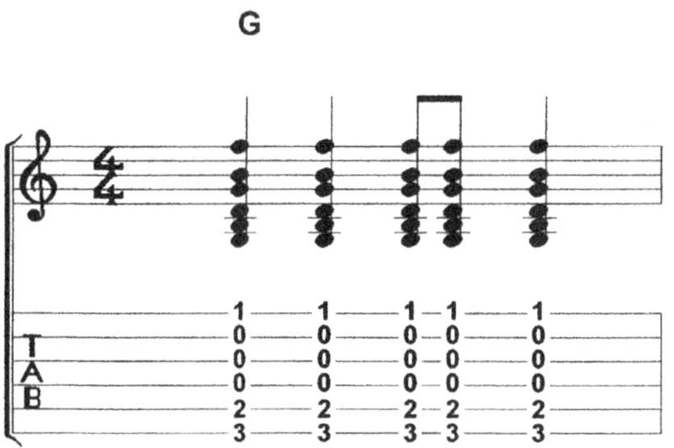

A fine rhythm here, and fairly interesting chords—particularly the shift to the D minor, which is unexpected after the standard C—F change. But what makes the track standout is the part that gets layered on top of this foundation. Consider the effect of punctuating the chord change with single, ringing chords on a second guitar:

Example 5.3

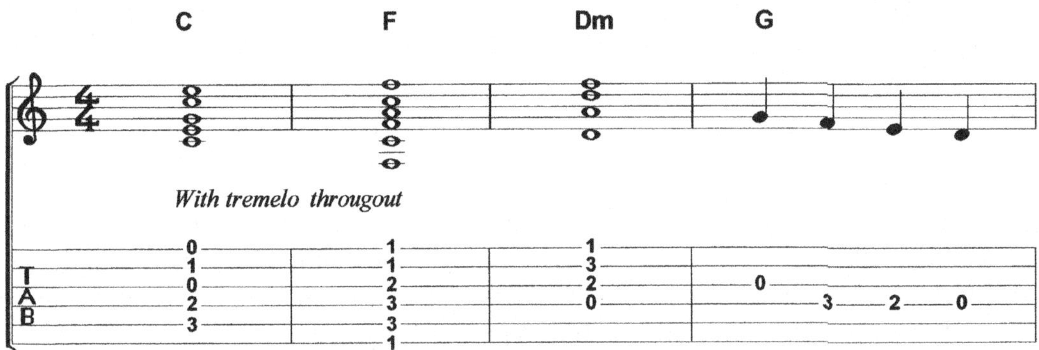

The run that begins in the fourth measure above lands firmly on a C note, sending us back to the beginning of the chord progression. On Williams' song, this second guitar happens to be an electric twelve-string played with moderate vibrato. But even hearing these parts on two acoustics would demonstrate how much texture you can add to a tune with well-thought out guitar lines. (If you don't have a multi-track recorder, you can tape the basic rhythm and then play along on the second guitar to hear this effect.)

And the result is even greater if you expand the possible voicings of the chords. Consider adding this part, for example:

Example 5.4

All fret positions relative to capo on the third fret

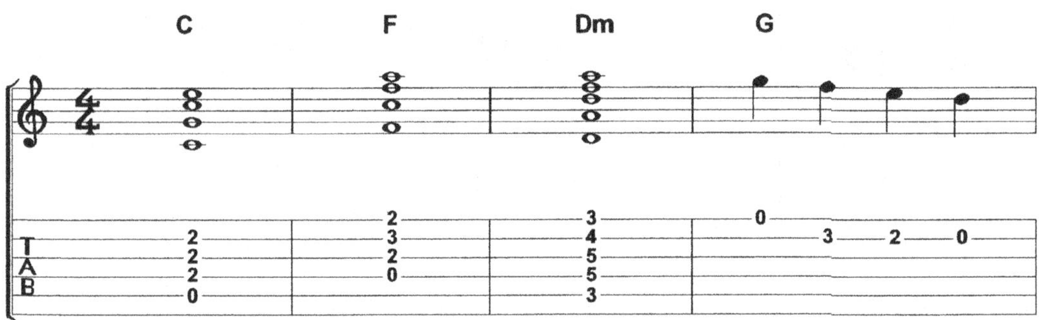

At this stage of composition, you want to pay attention not just to the structure of the song, but to how it sounds when it's played. When you strap a capo on the neck and play the chords outlined above, you give the song a unique timbre: such shifts can subtly and sometimes even dramatically alter the composition. Creating such an individual style is what you should aim for in every part of every song you write.

As you begin to study arrangements, you might also listen to bands that resist the strummed guitar part altogether: think of the Smiths or RE.M. or U.2. These bands rely on strong, almost lead-like bass lines to hold their tunes together. Then on top of that solid foundation, the guitar is free to play melodic lines, double stops, or pedal tones—parts that you might assume could not be done in bands with a single guitar player.

Keep in mind that the best parts to a song often pass by our conscious attention. They are so carefully crafted, and so subtly integrated into the piece that we're left with an indelible musical impression—but we sometimes remain unaware of the origins of that impression. In other words, we often don't hear as much as feel the parts that define a song. Crafting such a part involves the art of understatement, one that makes a hero-ic demand on the average guitarist: move beyond your ego. The song isn't about you or your guitar part; the song is bigger than any individual player.

My favorite example of this kind of craftsmanship occurs on the Beatles' track "Ticket to Ride." The opening lick has a brittle, almost distorted tone supported by an inventive tom-tom run and thrumming bass line. But if you listen to the riff and the verse carefully, you'll hear something interesting: one lone guitar plucking a single whole note on the open A string at the beginning of every measure. It looks something like this:

Example 5.5

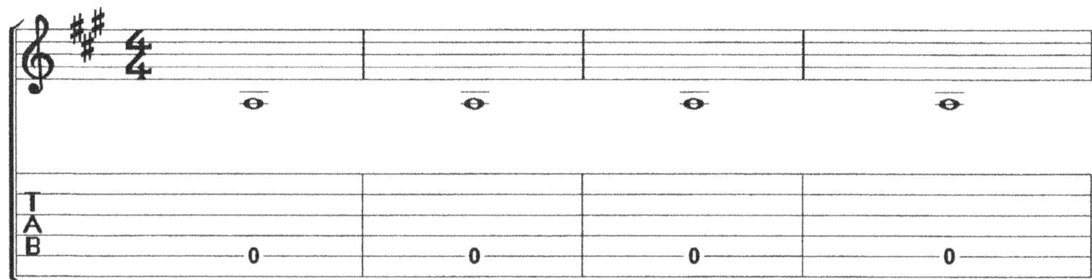

I suggest that you put the cd on and play along with that guitar track many times. You'll soon get the idea: whoever handled that job was not basking in the spotlight a la Hendrix. But the bottom note adds crucial depth to the piercing chime of the riff. Subtract it, and you've lost part of what defines the tune. Again, this is not a part that stands out or that you would ever have cause to hear unless you were dissecting the Beatles' art. This guitar line suggests how they created it, one part at a time.

Another great example of perfectly simple, perfectly apt guitar part occurs in the B-52's song "Private Idaho." Here the main riff is a fairly simple one played on the low E string, rising rapidly from an E to a G before landing on an A note. Above this jagged bass run, a second guitar pokes through with sharp notes played on the higher strings. It initially sets up an ascending riff, not unlike this one:

Example 5.6

Then the guitar settles down to play a high E note after each repetition of the main riff, alternately plucking it once and then twice throughout the verses:

Example 5.7

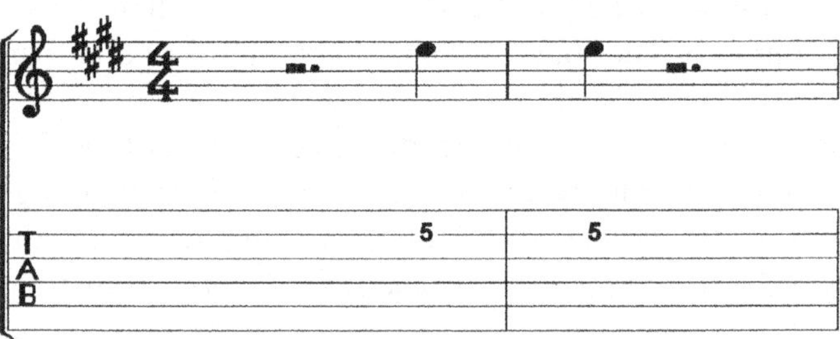

Literally anyone who picked up a guitar for the first time could learn this part without much difficulty. But it's tailored for the song, and adds to the frenzied lurch in the rhythm.

So when you're tempted to think that you need to play fast, complicated riffs to dazzle everyone, remind yourself of these examples. The parts work together to build the song, and each one, no matter how small, can help create the larger impression you seek.

Three Keys to the City

While listening to classic records and training yourself to pay attention to the arrangement, here are some elements to listen for that could give your songs definition, so that each part makes a contribution:

Dynamics

In many, many bands, every member plays at full volume for every song, the only break occurring when the guitarist stomps on a distortion pedal for a solo. This love affair with loudness is a point of pride for many bands, who believe that if a fan still has any hearing left after a gig they have somehow failed. But even most hardcore bands have a more subtle approach. The immediate example that comes to mind is Nirvana. Kurt Cobain received accolades for his soft verse/loud chorus approach, which added depth and emotional intensity to his songs. Think of it this way: if you scream all the time, no one will know when you're really mad. The same holds for the emotion of a song. If you play as loud as you can for the entire tune, no part will be emphasized, and no emotion will be underscored.

Cobain obviously drew on a long history of thrashy underground music for inspiration. If you want to hear one major influence, listen to the Pixies—especially a track such as "Gigantic" from *Surfer Rosa*. The band lulls you into complacency with a soft melody over a pulsing bass and drum line, only to launch into a frenzied romp through the chorus.

Such dramatic shifts in volume, of course, have by now become a kind of cliché for so-called alternative bands. But the lesson remains worth considering: pay attention to the dynamics of your song. Figure out which sections should be downplayed through a shift in volume, and consider how the guitar could lay back on certain parts to achieve a compelling effect. Then when you really want to play loudly, it will have an impact.

Tone & Style

Read any biography of the Beatles, and it will tell you how the band constantly sought to redefine the sound of their instruments and voices as they moved into their classic studio period. Their main producer, George Martin, tells stories of their repeated requests to make the guitar sound like a piano, or an organ, or a saxophone. Listen to the fuzz guitar lick at the opening of "Happiness is a Warm Gun," for example—consider the ingenuity it took to compose and play a line that sounds so much like a sax. And of course, songs such as "I'm only Sleeping," "Tomorrow Never Knows," and "Rain" all incorporated some element of backwards recording.

In a more contemporary vein, John Frusciante received much acclaim for his early work with the Red Hot Chili Peppers and the Hendrix-esque strat sound that he employed on songs such as "Under the Bridge." But for the band's album *By the Way,* he claimed that he was growing tired of the classic sound he had so thoroughly mastered. He wanted to challenge himself and set out in a new direction, and one way he did so was by composing parts on the guitar as though it were a keyboard. If you listen to tracks such as "By the Way" and "Universally Speaking," for example, you can hear how Frusciante consciously moves beyond the patterns and scales of blues-based rock guitar playing. Such an approach not only refreshes the musical style of your material, but also helps you push yourself to new levels as a player.

Here's a riff similar to the opening of "By the Way" that signals this shift in Frusciante's playing:

Example 5.8

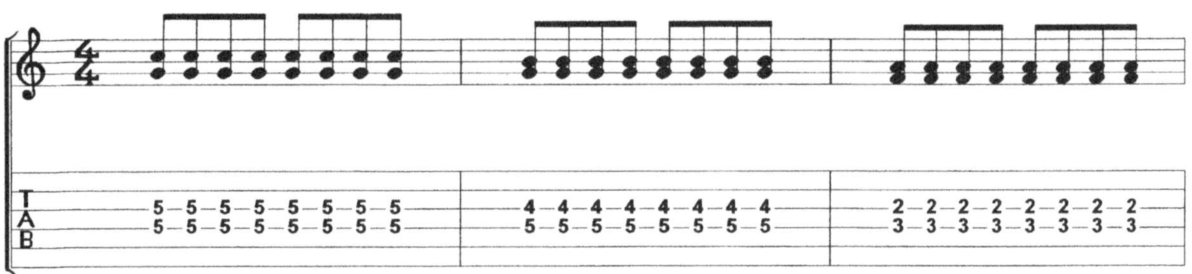

Played with all down-strokes, this guitar line sets an original tone with its insistent eighth-note rhythm and descending bass line. In fact, those two qualities are what make the riff akin to a piano part—particularly with the inversion of the C chord in the first measure, employing a G note on the bottom and a C note above it. Guitar players don't often employ such inversions, so they stand out when you hear them. Moreover, the G and F chords employ an unusual interval of a third, which makes the drop from the F to the D so interesting as the part moves to the last measure. In his playing, Frusciante uses similar tactics to add a distinctive, often melancholic feel to his band's songs.

The message is don't just plug in and play. Refuse to take anything for granted with your own songs as you consciously look for new styles, tones, rhythms, intervals, etc. Adopting an attitude of restless experimentation as you approach each piece of music, ask yourself how you can transform your sound to make each song memorable.

Rhythm and Pacing

Another element to consider when arranging guitar parts concerns the rhythm. Here you can ask the same question I posed about volume: do you play every part of the song in the same rhythm, with the same strumming or picking pattern? If so, start paying attention to the songs you love and note where the tempo and rhythm vary. For a classic example, consider Led Zeppelin's "Livin', Lovin' Maid (She's Just a Woman)," as it shifts to the halting D—A—D—E chord changes for the bridge, before driving back into the propulsive guitar line of the verse. In a more contemporary vein, listen again to Hole's "Celebrity Skin," with it's ironic, upbeat bridge marking a sharp turn from the jagged guitar lines of the verse. In a three-minute song, changes like this add depth and work to hold the listener's attention.

For other kinds of variations, look to songs that include transitions between fingerpicking and strumming. John Frusciante is a master of this: listen to songs such as "Under the Bridge" and "Scar Tissue," in which he deftly moves from plucking the strings to full strumming. Again, such shifts can give your song immense depth—they suggest a sophisticated, highly refined arrangement, and add nuance to what would otherwise be a one-dimensional tune.

Finally, when polishing your own composition, you might look for places where the band can stop together. A dramatic pause adds its own kind of tension to an arrangement, and often grabs your ear as much as the loudest guitar fusillade.

Double Your Pleasure

One common technique for recording is to double a singer's voice, which gives it a depth and power that it sometimes lacks as a solo performance. But the same tactic can also help other instruments—and it can be used not only for recording, but also for live gigs if you have the right combination of musicians in your band.

Consider combining these instruments as they play the same part:
- an electric guitar with an acoustic guitar
- a bass guitar part with a piano
- a bass guitar line with a guitar
- any two distinct instruments

One classic example of the power of doubling occurs in the Beatles' "Day Tripper." The opening guitar and bass lines in E are actually not an octave apart (the way that some cover bands lamely play it). By keeping guitar and bass in the same register at the start, the riff takes on a powerful resonance that leaves your speakers humming. While doubling guitars can create a strong effect, it's the last suggestion here—doubling two very distinct instruments—that allows your creativity to shine: by doing so, you can employ two well-known instruments to create a vivid new sound. Examples of this abound on the Beach Boys' *Pet Sounds,* on which Brian Wilson combined a bass harmonica with a bass guitar, for example, and as standard practice doubled the electric bass with a stand-up bass. Although you might not have access to such an array of equipment (or studio musicians), you can always rely on a synthesizer or guitar effects pedal to simulate other compelling tones.

If you're recording, keeping the two parts in the same spot on the stereo spectrum melds them together to help create a new or unusual tone, while separating the parts gives depth and add interest to them. As always, experiment—especially in the mix—to find the sound that works best for the song.

All Things Counter, Original, Spare, Strange

By this point, the premise of the book should be plain: attempt something you've never done before in every song you write. Aim for a new sound, a different kind of intro, an unusual tuning, a striking combination of instruments, an anti-hero solo—whatever it is, simply be sure you have not tried it before. No surprise for you when you compose it, no surprise for the listener who hears it.

As you cultivate surprise in your compositions, consider one final point about originality and arrangements: most guitar players play too much. You don't want to be one of those guitarists who strum too many tepid chords and meander too long with ill-considered solos. There is a lot to be said for reticence, for holding back, for playing the right note at the right time.

Recall the example of Eric Clapton when he heard the Band's first record, *Music from Big Pink*. Stunned by the effect that Robbie Robertson achieved with such unaffected playing, Clapton claims that the record ultimately helped change the direction of his career—he moved beyond Cream and the wild, distortion-driven excesses of acid rock eventually to produce his masterpiece, *Layla and Other Love Songs*. On that album, he shares lead duties with Duane Allman and often takes a less-is-more approach to playing that emphasizes song-craft over pyrotechnics.

As Clapton's example suggests, you need to keep listening, experimenting, and learning as you develop your unique songwriting style as a guitarist—and for the greatest artists, that development never stops. If you pursue your craft with such dedication, you're sure to produce compelling songs that you can be proud of and that someone else will want to sing and play.

Exercises

1) Consider the tone of your guitar part. What could you do to make it sound less like a conventional guitar? You might start with various foot-pedals or effects, but also think about how to use these pedals in unusual ways. For example, Frank Zappa often soloed with his wah-wah pedal depressed half-way. Instead of getting the classic "wacha-wacha" sound by rocking on the pedal, he gave his riffs a strangely compressed, entirely original timbre. Play with the effects until you find a sound that you feel is compelling—and let this tone inspire you to come up with a new riff.

2) Try to write a part for your song on the guitar as though it were another instrument. For starters, consider the John Frusciante example above, and play it like a keyboard. But don't be afraid to imagine weirder alternatives: How could your guitar sound like a saxophone, a marimba—or a tuba?

3) Consider ways of physically modifying your guitar. What would it sound like if you wove a piece of paper through your strings? Or put electrical tape across them? Or used a sponge (dry, please!) as a damper underneath them? Also, how would it sound if you played with a coin instead of a pick?

4) Compose a basic chord sequence for a song and then record it. Don't worry about making it overly original at this point, and simply strum the rhythm so that you've got a solid base to work with. Now keeping the above example of multiple chord positions in mind, play along with your track as you experiment with different voicings. Listen for the way these voicings change the mood or feel of the piece—and can possibly transform the progression into an original part for a song.

4) Using a song that you have already composed, consider five alternative ways to open it: for example, a drum lick, a bass run, a startling chord (a bass chord?), an unusual guitar effect, or any other surprising way to catch the listener's attention. Don't settle for what you already have in mind or how you think the song

"should" go; try to remain open to the multitude of options you really have.

5) When you're introducing the song to your band and beginning to rehearse it, make a point of stopping to ask for input from the other musicians. Although it's sometimes difficult to let others help shape what started as a very private creation, any one of your bandmates could offer an insight to help take the song further than you might have imagined. A good band should help you see further possibilities in your music; when such collaboration works, it can lead to far better songs.

6) Take one of your songs apart section by section, and ask what makes each one distinct. Consider whether you're strumming through generic chord changes in standard positions for the entire piece (and then ask yourself whether you even need to play guitar for the whole song). If you want to make the guitar track more interesting, think about how you can vary the rhythm or chord voicing or picking pattern or tone or volume to set each section apart. And listen to the band as well—how are they working together to accentuate the changes in the song?

7) When rehearsing the song, listen carefully to all the parts. Is everyone playing at full volume for the whole song? Why? Is it necessary? Does it fit the composition? Consider ways to vary the dynamics of the song by making one or more instruments quieter during one verse or on the bridge.

8) Without worrying too much about the quality of the recording, tape your song on a multi-track recorder, giving an individual track to each instrument in your band. Then later, play the song back, isolating the tracks, and listen to each one with your full attention. Ask yourself two things: a) Is the part interesting in itself? Sometimes a vibrantly strummed acoustic makes a song, but you'll likely find a dull guitar part in at least one section; and b) How does each part, interesting as it might be, contribute to the song as a whole? In short, you want to be sure that it sounds like you are performing the song as a band, not as a bunch of loosely connected individuals.

9) When you've got a collection of songs together, listen to them as a group, with an ear toward the sound you are creating as a band. Do you always use the same instruments, through the same amps, with the same settings, played in the same style on every song? Of course you want your material to sound as though it belongs together. But you also need to give each piece distinctive features that set it apart.

10) Without thinking too much about it, make a short list of songs you love to play, either alone or with your band. Now quickly jot down beside each one what it is that makes it so fun for you. After you have identified these qualities, ask yourself whether they are reflected in your own songs. If not, consider ways that you can add similar parts to your material. For example, it's really fun to play lead parts in unison with another guitar (even if they're short or mark a transition to the chorus, etc.). What would make another guitar player think that your song was that interesting?

11) When thinking of ways to vary your sound, don't forget to explore alternative tunings. Can you use drop D tuning or an open tuning for any of your songs? If you're feeling stuck or uninspired in your writing, learn a new tuning or invent one of your own—then compose a song with it.

Appendix A: Further Reading

Here's a list of books for further reading. Some are about guitar playing, some about creativity in general, and some about stretching your creative abilities in ways you might not have considered. Each asks you to think in different ways about your art—and possibly about yourself as an artist:

Drawing on the Right Side of the Brain by Betty Edwards (Tarcher).
> Yes, this is a book about drawing. But the exercises in it are so intriguing that they will make you literally see the world differently—especially if you think you have no talent as a visual artist. That alone is a deep source of inspiration.

Creating Minds: An Anatomy of Creativity Seen Through the Lives of Freud, Einstein, Picasso, Stravinsky, Eliot, Graham, and Gandhi by Howard Gardner (Basic Books).
> A great book for those who want an in-depth treatment of issues surrounding creativity by one of the leading researchers in the field. Although the introductory theory is complex, the chapters on innovative people offer reader-friendly stories about powerful, creative lives.

A Hard Day's Write: The Stories Behind Every Beatles' Song by Steve Turner (Harper).
> A trove of details about the most famous song catalog in rock history. The book identifies the inspiration for many of the songs, and presents John and Paul in particular as working writers who drew from their experience. If they could be inspired by newspaper articles or the peculiar people they encountered, why can't you?

Mindfulness by Ellen Langer (Addison Wesley).
> Not a book about guitar playing or creativity per se, Langer's work nonetheless explains how our mindless routines and habits lead us to constricted thinking. The way out of this straight jacket—and the way to creativity in all areas of life—is through mindfulness, or focused attention on our experiences as we have them.

The Playboy Interviews with John Lennon and Yoko Ono by John Lennon, Yoko Ono, David Sheff, and G. Barry Golson (Putnam).
> This is the bible in terms of Lennon's candid description of his songwriting partnership with Paul McCartney: who wrote what, how they wrote it, and what he thought about the songs at the time of the interview, shortly before his death.

Secrets from the Masters: Conversations with Forty Great Guitar Players by Don Menn (Backbeat Books).
> A great book about guitar playing in which you learn fascinating technical details about how some of rock's best players put together their sound and style. Covers everyone from Chuck Berry and Keith Richards to Eddie Van Halen and Steve Vai.

Songwriters on Songwriting by Paul Zollo (Da Capo Press).
> In this collection, a veteran journalist presents his interviews with an impressive list of rock songwriters. We hear from a wide array of artists, including Neil Young, Frank Zappa, Carlos Santana, and k.d. lang.

Written in My Soul: Conversations with Rock's Great Songwriters by Bill Flanagan (Contemporary Books).
> An insightful book offering interviews with a host of rock's most original and enduring songwriters, including Bob Dylan, Joni Mitchell, and David Byrne. Candid and focused, these interviews really do center on the craft of writing songs, and they reveal the stunning variety of approaches taken by many of the greats.

Zen Guitar by Philip Toshio Sudo (Simon and Schuster).

The only philosophical book about guitar playing that I've seen—and it's a great one. The book contains no literal music lessons, scales, or chord charts. But Sudo leads you to think about your playing in an entirely new light, with a focus on the habits of mind that can help you enrich your practice and performance no matter what your current ability.

Appendix B: Guide to Tablature

The tablature in this book generally reflects standard practice in contemporary guitar books and magazines. If you have no trouble reading them, you will have no trouble here. Below, I lay out some of the basic concepts and explain the key symbols that might be helpful in reading this music.

APPENDIX B TABLATURE

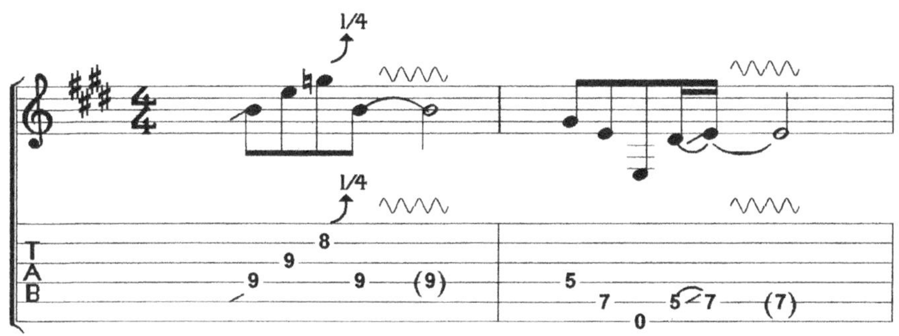

The six guitar strings are represented from low to high as you move from the bottom to the top of the tab lines. The numbers on the tab lines indicate where the notes should be fretted. In terms of symbols, an up-turned arrow indicates a bend, and the percentage above it identifies the extent of the bend (e.g., 1/4 = a one-quarter note bend). A wavy line above a note means that it is played with strong vibrato. Other common symbols include the following:

H = Hammer-on
P = Pull-off
/ = Slide

Any special tuning or performance notes are included as text lines before or within the tablature.

UNIQUELY INTERESTING MUSIC!

Made in the USA
Monee, IL
07 July 2026

56552246R00033